# The Netherworld in Ancient Egypt and China

Also Available from Bloomsbury:

*Ancient Egyptian Scribes*, Niv Allon and Hana Navratilova
*Five Egyptian Goddesses*, Susan Tower Hollis
*A Brief History of Ancient China*, Edward L. Shaughnessy

# The Netherworld in Ancient Egypt and China

*An Imagined Paradise*

Mu-chou Poo

BLOOMSBURY ACADEMIC
LONDON • NEW YORK • OXFORD • NEW DELHI • SYDNEY

BLOOMSBURY ACADEMIC

Bloomsbury Publishing Plc, 50 Bedford Square, London, WC1B 3DP, UK
Bloomsbury Publishing Inc, 1385 Broadway, New York, NY 10018, USA
Bloomsbury Publishing Ireland, 29 Earlsfort Terrace, Dublin 2, D02 AY28, Ireland

BLOOMSBURY, BLOOMSBURY ACADEMIC and the Diana logo are trademarks of
Bloomsbury Publishing Plc

First published in Great Britain 2024
Paperback edition published 2025

Copyright © Mu-chou Poo, 2024

Mu-chou Poo has asserted their right under the Copyright, Designs and Patents Act, 1988,
to be identified as Author of this work.

Cover design: Rebecca Heselton
Cover image : Sennedjem and lineferti in the Fields of Iaru ca. 1295–1213 B.C. Tempera
on paper. H. 54 cm x W. 84.5 cm. © Rogers Fund, 1930, Met Museum

All rights reserved. No part of this publication may be: i) reproduced or transmitted
in any form, electronic or mechanical, including photocopying, recording or by means
of any information storage or retrieval system without prior permission in writing from
the publishers; or ii) used or reproduced in any way for the training, development or
operation of artificial intelligence (AI) technologies, including generative AI technologies.
The rights holders expressly reserve this publication from the text and data mining
exception as per Article 4(3) of the Digital Single Market Directive (EU) 2019/790.

Bloomsbury Publishing Plc does not have any control over, or responsibility for, any
third-party websites referred to or in this book. All internet addresses given in this
book were correct at the time of going to press. The author and publisher regret any
inconvenience caused if addresses have changed or sites have ceased to exist,
but can accept no responsibility for any such changes.

A catalogue record for this book is available from the British Library.

A catalog record for this book is available from the Library of Congress.

ISBN: HB: 978-0-5677-0200-5
PB: 978-0-5677-0204-3
ePDF: 978-0-5677-0201-2
eBook: 978-0-5677-0203-6

Typeset by Newgen KnowledgeWorks Pvt. Ltd., Chennai, India

For product safety related questions contact productsafety@bloomsbury.com.

To find out more about our authors and books visit www.bloomsbury.com
and sign up for our newsletters.

# Contents

| | | |
|---|---|---|
| List of Illustrations | | vi |
| Chronology | | vii |
| Preface | | viii |
| 1 | Introduction | 1 |
| 2 | The Evolution of Burial Style and the Imagination of the Netherworld | 13 |
| 3 | Iconographic Representations of the Netherworld | 37 |
| 4 | Textual Representations of the Netherworld | 61 |
| 5 | Belief, Ethics, and the Life Hereafter | 87 |
| 6 | Hope, Fear, and the Quest for Happiness | 109 |
| 7 | Conclusion | 135 |
| References | | 145 |
| Index | | 157 |

# Illustrations

| | | |
|---|---|---|
| 2.1 | An idealized drawing of the mastaba | 16 |
| 2.2 | A typical mastaba | 17 |
| 2.3 | Rock-cut tombs | 18 |
| 2.4 | Idealized line-drawing of a vertical-pit wooden-casket tomb | 27 |
| 2.5 | A rock-cut tomb at Beidongshan, Western Han period | 29 |
| 2.6 | A typical brick tomb | 31 |
| 3.1 | Tomb of Mereruka | 40 |
| 3.2 | Representation of the Field of Offering in the tomb of Sennedjem | 43 |
| 3.3 | A slaughterhouse | 45 |
| 3.4 | The T-shaped painting on silk from Mawangdui tomb no. 1 | 48 |
| 3.5 | A fragment of a boating scene on a silk cloth found in Mawangdui tomb no. 3 | 52 |
| 3.6 | A silk painting found in an early Han tomb discovered at Jinqueshan, Linyi | 53 |

# Chronology

## Ancient Egypt

Early Dynastic period: c. 3100–2686 BCE
Old Kingdom period: c. 2686–2181 BCE
First Intermediate period: c. 2181–2055 BCE
Middle Kingdom period: c. 2125–1773 BCE
Second Intermediate period: c. 1773–1550 BCE
New Kingdom period: c. 1550–1069 BCE
Third Intermediate period: c. 1069–715 BCE
Late Period: c. 715–332 BCE
Ptolemaic Dynasty: 304–30 BCE
Roman Period: 30 BCE–304 CE

## Ancient China

Shang Dynasty: c. 1600–1046 BCE
Western Zhou Dynasty: c. 1042–722 BCE
Eastern Zhou Dynasty: c. 722–256 BCE
Spring and Autumn period: 722–453 BCE
Warring States period: 453–221 BCE
Qin Dynasty: 221–207 BCE
Han Dynasty: 202 BCE–220 CE

# Preface

This book is a token of appreciation of my good fortune in a long pursuit of something beyond personal capability. Trained as an Egyptologist, I did not follow a traditional path of Egyptological study, but from early on ventured into comparative study, perhaps due to my personal background as someone who had studied Chinese history before turning to Egypt. I have tried to find ways to look at history from a comparative point of view, because it is my belief that "one who knows one, knows none." It could have begun with a very simple wish to know more about history, or histories, to find out how and why people and culture differed from each other. But as time goes by, this simple wish becomes more difficult to fulfill. It might be relatively easy to find out how cultures differ, but why? And what do the differences and similarities mean? This book is an attempt at finding some answers to this simple wish, by investigating a theme common to all human societies, that is, death and the netherworld. It is also an attempt at using comparison as a method to approach different cultures and hoping to come up with some fresh ways to understand these cultures as well as humanities in general. I tried to make a connection between the idea of the netherworld with people's pursuit of happiness and argue that one way to understand the idea of the netherworld was to see it as a product of the pursuit of happiness. This allows me to engage in a more complex crisscross comparison, of ancient Egypt and early China, on the issues related to the netherworld and happiness. The end result, as presented in this book, is now ready for examination by interested readers. Needless to say, but one says it anyway, this book only serves as an example of comparative studies that does not purport to provide any definitive answer. However, by being an example, it may provide some concrete evidence of how comparison should or should not be done. One person's blunders may be many conscientious readers' opportunities.

This book is dedicated to my family. To Cindy and Sheila who observed my work with strong interest, as I observed theirs. To Ping-chen who provided unfailing love and support, to which I could not find a suitable expression but to say next time I will try to be better.

1

# Introduction

## The Aim of This Study

Throughout history, most societies have in one way or another suffered from various kinds of destructions and desolations, yet the urge and determination to seek happiness—however defined—was a universal phenomenon that sustained and gave nourishment to the development of each society. As happiness was often elusive, in fact usually difficult to achieve,[1] some societies resorted to constructing an ideal existence beyond this life on earth—a paradise, or a netherworld, based on their earthly experience, their aspirations and apprehensions, as well as their hopes for a rewarding future life. The interrelationship between the concept of the netherworld, the belief system, and the social norms that formulated the idea of happiness, therefore, may provide researchers with insights into a particular cultural system. Moreover, since these are issues common to most societies and cultures, the significance of one example could best be illustrated by reference to another.

Inspired by these considerations, this study aims at investigating the relationship between the idea of the netherworld and the search for happiness from a comparative perspective that draws upon examples from Pharaonic Egypt (c. 3100–30 BCE) and ancient China (c. 1600 BCE–220 CE).

Many parallels existed between ancient Egypt and ancient China, one of which was the belief in a netherworld. While the imagined netherworlds of these two societies differed in their details, they nevertheless shared a common source of inspiration, namely that they were drawn from and shaped by a fundamental crave for survival and a collective urge to seek for a postmortem existence. This study will compare the core values of each society in order to establish to what extent beliefs and values related to religion, ethics, and the nature of happiness were present in ancient Chinese and Egyptian visions of life after death.

---

[1] See McMahon (2006).

While ancient Egypt had been studied extensively, a comparative approach had rarely been conducted, particularly one such as the present book, which roots the imagination of the netherworld in the experience of daily life. The structural similarities between these two civilizations, each with rich funerary traditions, suggest that profitable comparison of the two cultures could yield mutually illuminating insights into their understanding of the meanings of life and happiness. By imagining and describing the netherworld, the ancient Egyptians and Chinese left for us traces of their beliefs about life.

What, then, is the relevance of an understanding of the ancient Egyptian or Chinese ideas of the netherworld to the intellectual concerns of our contemporary society? The answer may lie in historical connections and universal human conditions. As Egypt and China (for the period treated in this project) are each in their world—Egypt in the pre-Christian West and China in pre-Buddhist East Asia—important cultural systems with a far-reaching influence on later historical developments in their respective world, any study of the fundamental issues of religion and culture (such as the netherworld) in later eras would be given a useful basis with this exercise of tracing the earlier phases of these issues and addressing their possible cultural configurations.

For example, in modern China, the continuous belief in the existence of the soul and the need to provide funerary objects for the deceased reflects an enduring fascination as well as anxiety concerning the afterlife. The emphasis on assisting the dead to pass through various difficulties in the netherworld and providing them with enough provision for a comfortable life through funerary rituals[2]—in a sense a preparation for eternal happiness—has existed in China as early as the pre-imperial period.[3] The religious mentality of our modern society, however it had changed or evolved, is firmly anchored in the past and needs to be understood in the context of this long tradition. Such enduring concern with life after death, moreover, suggests strongly that what we observe is not limited to the here and now, but is a manifestation of some common human conditions, which could be demonstrated, firstly, by considering practices elsewhere in earlier times and, secondly, by comparison with significant examples such as the ancient Egyptian idea of the netherworld.

In fact, for a civilization as early as ancient Egypt, most surviving sources are related to religious beliefs. These sources may present a skewed view of the Egyptian experience as being overwhelmingly religious. Nevertheless it

---

[2] Watson and Rawski (1988).
[3] Poo (1998).

is through the study of them that our understanding of Egyptian culture and society was based upon. The netherworld, being one of the central concerns in the belief system of not only ancient Egypt, but many societies, as it touches upon issues of belief, ethics, and social life, was such a prominent subject that no study of Egyptian religion and society could afford to ignore. The search for eternal happiness, moreover, features prominently in Egyptian funerary practice and religious literature. In particular, the Egyptians believed in the existence of three different souls, representing different aspects of the life force of a person,[4] while the extensive burial customs, with all the ritual paraphernalia, were comparable to ancient Chinese funerary practice. A case could be made in seeing a structural comparability between the two.

One of the goals of this study, therefore, will be to demonstrate, with concrete examples, that thematic comparison of ancient civilizations is not only possible, but relevant to modern society. The concept of the commonality of humanity becomes a basis used to decipher cultural differences. Through comparison, we learn that such differences can be traced back to how people in different historical and cultural contexts managed to deal with universal human problems in their own fashion.

It is a fact of humanity that human imagination, despite its capacity to create new things that had not existed before, still relies heavily on previous experience that the mind had absorbed during its life course whether as a person or society at large. Arguably, all human creations are built on previous knowledge and cumulated imagination in one way or another and in different combinations and syntheses. Our analysis of the ideas of the netherworld in ancient Egypt and China will therefore be based on this assumption. Since no one has returned from the netherworld, all the descriptions of it are necessarily constructed based on the life experience of the people in these ancient societies and reconstructed by the modern researcher.

## An Overview of the Subject

The prominent position of the netherworld in both Egypt and early China, which constitutes the main subject of the present book, is built on the fact that in these two early civilizations, especially Egypt, sources of religious nature have survived more than any other. It was in the mid-nineteenth century that the Egyptian idea

---

[4] Eyre (2009); Poo (2022b, chapter 7).

of the netherworld began to be noticed when the importance of the *Book of the Dead* was recognized.⁵ The discovery of two other types of religious texts in late nineteenth century, namely the *Pyramid Texts*⁶ and the *Coffin Texts*,⁷ provide us with more evidence of the Egyptian perceptions of the netherworld. Notably, it became known that the whereabouts of the netherworld changed several times in the course of Egyptian history, from heaven to the Eastern Horizon, then to the West. To a certain extent, this shift had to do with sociopolitical changes over time.

Since the mid-twentieth century, the subject of the netherworld continued to receive attention, as almost all scholarly discussions of Egyptian religion touched upon this subject.⁸ A number of studies dealt with particular versions of the netherworld such as the Field of Rushes and the Field of Offerings.⁹ However, most discussion of the netherworld focuses on the fate awaiting the dead and, above all, on the relationship between the idea of the netherworld and the judgment after death that the deceased had to go through. As such, the concept of the netherworld was mostly discussed in the context of justice, morality, and death.¹⁰

Relatively less attention, however, has been given to detailed reconstruction of the overall conception of this netherworld (or netherworlds) based on archaeological finds such as tomb paintings and funerary objects. There is also a need for an in-depth study of the relationship between the concept of the netherworld and the secular values and life experience of the people who created it. In other words, the reason why the ancient Egyptians portrayed the netherworld the way they did should be explained in light of the religious system that created the netherworld, and the social values of the living who had created and supported the religious systems in the first place. For example, as M. Lichtheim pointed out, one aspect of happiness that the Egyptians recognized was the possession of material goods and the enjoyment of food and drink.¹¹ Such conduits to happiness found their expression in funerary customs, since the Egyptians believed that a good burial must include food and drink if it was to be a springboard into a happy afterlife.¹² As such, and admittedly a rather banal

---

⁵ Naville (1886).
⁶ Maspero (1893); Sethe (1908–22).
⁷ Lacau (1910); de Buck (1935–61).
⁸ Kees ([1926] 1983); Morenz (1973); Hornung (1982); Baines (1991); Hornung (1999); Assmann (2002).
⁹ Lesko (1971–2); Leclant (1975); Hays (2015).
¹⁰ Jacq (1986); Hornung (1982: 60–2).
¹¹ Lichtheim (1997: 50–8).
¹² Richards (2005).

representation, the conception of the netherworld was built upon an embedded assumption about what happiness was consisted of and how happiness could be attained in the netherworld, with burial a medium or a passage leading toward that state of happiness. As often mentioned in the *Book of the Dead*, the deceased, after passing the test of innocence before Osiris, the Lord of the netherworld, could finally enter the "Beautiful West," where they would know only eternal happiness. The worldly search for happiness was in this sense intimately connected with the vision of the netherworld.

By comparison, the study of the ancient Chinese conception of the netherworld in modern scholarship can be traced to the early twentieth century when the French Sinologist E. Chavannes published his study of Mont Tai, the location where, during the Han Dynasty, all ghosts were thought to gather.[13] However, Chavannes's study was long preceded by the late Ming and early Qing Dynasty scholar Gu Yanwu (1613–1682) who had collected most of the important textual evidence on Mount Tai as the place where the ghosts gathered, therefore the equivalent of a netherworld.[14] Scholars have since come to view Mount Tai as where the world of the dead was located in pre-Buddhist China.[15] There are also other conceptions of the world after death in early China since the Warring States period, such as the Yellow Spring (*Huangquan*), the Dark City (*Youdu*), or simply the Underground (*dixia*).[16] The general picture is that, in ancient China, before the arrival of Buddhism, there appeared to be no unified concept of the netherworld, as different views coexisted side by side. Some of these conceptions of the netherworld may not be particularly well articulated. The Yellow Spring, for example, is most likely a metaphorical expression of the netherworld, probably originated from the fact that yellowish underground water gushed out during the excavation of the grave pit in places where underground water level was high.[17] The Dark City, by contrast, is a place with no light whatsoever, where monstrous animals/deities dwell. In the Han Dynasty, the simple and straightforward term "Underground" emerged as a designation for the netherworld, and people also imagined this underground world in accordance with their experiences on earth, or at least partially so. For example, the deceased would need to pay taxes to the underground government

---

[13] Chavannes (1910).
[14] Gu (1970: 877).
[15] Yu (1987); Liu (1997).
[16] Pirazzoli-T'Serstevens (2009).
[17] Wu Hung (2010).

and to report their addresses to the underground local magistrates, just as they needed to do when alive.[18]

The imagination of the world after death in early China can thus be understood as unsystematic, or multifaceted, since there was no dominating ideology to limit the imagination. The guiding principle, if there was one, had to do with the fate of the deceased in the netherworld and the concerns about providing the deceased with the wherewithal for happiness, however vaguely conceived. This connection between the conception of the netherworld and the idea of happiness, with rare exceptions,[19] has not attracted much scholarly attention, presumably because traditionally the netherworld was discussed in the context of religious beliefs, while happiness was considered a subject for philosophy or ethics. However, happiness is a fundamental concern in human society not the least in ancient China and as such is pivotal to this study.[20]

## Comparative Study: Why and How

Since this study purports to approach the issue of the netherworld and the search for happiness from a comparative angle, some methodological issues need to be addressed—foremost among them are the theoretical foundation for comparative study and the practical method to be employed. With regard to theoretical considerations, the present book subscribes to the position that the goal of comparison should be more than discovering similarities and differences; it should result in mutually illuminating understanding of the subjects under comparison. We are seeking to gain fresh insights into the cultures that nurtured or produced the specific subjects in question, in this case the what and why of the formation of the conception of the netherworld. One can even say that the goal of comparison lies beyond the immediate subjects themselves, for they are but manifestations of their cultural foundations, and comparison, one way or another, seeks to illuminate such cultural foundations by positioning the compared against each other.

While the comparative study of ancient Egypt and China is a relatively new area of research, recent scholarship has begun to pay more attention to this area. I have made a series of investigations of the theme of the attitudes toward

---

[18] Loewe (1979); Seidel (1987).
[19] Bauer (1976).
[20] Jones (1953); Wierzbica (2004); McMahon (2006).

foreigners in ancient Egypt, Mesopotamia, and China.[21] One observation from this study is that people in the ancient world might have prejudice against the foreigners, yet unlike modern racism this prejudice was based mostly on cultural difference rather than racial difference. And we should also recognize that there was a disparity between the official ideology and the private sentiment, so at least we should guard against over-simplification in our presentation of an image of "the Egyptian" or "the Chinese" way of thinking. I have also compared the Egyptian Ushabti with the lead figure found in some Han Dynasty tombs,[22] as well as the conception of reverence toward the elders found in Egyptian Wisdom Literature and ancient Chinese text.[23] These studies in one way or another prepared the path for the present book.

A recent publication that may usher more comparative works is Anthony Barbieri-Low's *Ancient Egypt and Early China: State, Society, and Culture*.[24] Barbieri-Low points out the why and how of comparative study of history and gives a very useful overview of the current state of comparative history in the areas of China/Greco-Roman and China/Egypt comparison, pointing out the possible methodological issues and emphasizing that comparison could and should be made according to appropriate scheme and historical developmental stages. Comparison between Greco-Roman antiquity and ancient China may seem a natural choice, especially between the Roman Empire and Han Dynasty, yet there is no reason to limit our inquiry to these two periods. One point worth mentioning is that comparison should be based on structural similarity, rather than chronological proximity. Thus in his book, the comparison was made between New Kingdom Egypt and Western Han China, since each of the two periods occupied a key structural position in the development of these two civilizations, and both shared some structural similarities in terms of geopolitical development, bureaucratic government operated by highly trained scribes/literary class, universal justice guaranteed by the ruler and dispensed through law court, as well as elaborate funerary culture with imaginary netherworlds.

One issue often encountered in comparative study of historical societies is what to compare and how to choose the time span for comparison. As Barbieri-Low already pointed out, there are a number of ways to look at this issue. Those who compare ancient Greece with Warring States China or the Roman Empire with Han China often also subscribe to the chronological proximity

---

[21] Poo (1994, 1998, 2005).
[22] Poo (2003). See Chapter 5.
[23] Poo (2011b).
[24] Barbieri-Low (2021).

of the periods in comparison.²⁵ Attempts have also been made comparing the Byzantine and the Tang Empires for the same reason.²⁶ Yet there is another angle to look at the issue of comparability. This is the idea that comparison of human societies should be based on the structural and developmental stages of the comparands, and so as long as there is a structural similarity that could be found in different societies, this could be a valid starting point for comparison. Chronological proximity was not relevant. This approach is represented by Bruce Trigger's work comparing seven ancient civilizations, which is a model for anthropologists and archaeologists.²⁷ Trigger's work was both inspiring and controversial. Inspiring because he was able to work out a systemic paradigm to map out a number of comparands for analyzing the seven ancient societies that he deemed comparable. Controversial because the scheme of his work was too vast, even with his erudition, for him to be able to have full control of all the details, especially regarding the complicated histories of societies such as China for which he had no first-hand linguistic capability.

In a recent publication, I have tried this structural approach to tackle the phenomenon of a new belief encountering an old society, namely early Christianity in Rome and early Buddhism in China, and to examine the challenges, responses, resistance and rejections, and accommodations that happened between the new and the old.²⁸ In the present study, I still believe that comparison based on structural similarity should be a fruitful path to follow. While this position follows Trigger's lead, there are still many hurdles that need to be crossed.

First, how to choose a major theme for comparison? In this study, as already mentioned, I have chosen the idea of the netherworld as a focal point. Since the idea of the netherworld was a structural nod in the understanding of both Egyptian and Chinese beliefs, it brings out the structural similarity of both religious systems. Yet there is still another problem: even if we do not think chronological proximity of the compared was important, we still need to decide which period of history should we compare. This is an often encountered issue in the study of ancient societies. When we say Egyptian religion, can we assume that there was something called "Egyptian religion" throughout Egyptian history? If there were constant variations throughout history, can we still

---

[25] For example, see Lloyd (1996, 2002, 2006, 2018); Raphals (1992, 2013); Shankman and Durrant (2000, 2002); Scheidel (2009, 2015); Mutschler (2008).
[26] De Ligt (2003).
[27] Trigger (2003).
[28] Poo, Drake, and Raphals (2017).

call these variations by the same term? In fact, the common practice among Egyptologists was taking an expedient position. Most will recognize that there was a distinctive Egyptian religion that could be applied to most of the Egyptian history, while not denying that periodic and local variations did exist. Since the present study focuses on the idea of the netherworld, we shall take the entire Pharaonic period (c. 3000–300 BCE) as belonging to a pristine Egyptian religious culture, with some core ideas regarding the divine world, the cosmic order, the pantheon, the existence of the souls of *ba*, *ka*, and *akh*, and the idea of the netherworld.

As for China, my chosen period of comparison begins from the Shang and ends with the Eastern Han (c. 1700 BCE–300 CE), which, because of the incursion of Buddhism and the rise of religious Daoism, marked a division in the development of Chinese belief system from a pristine one to a synthetic one.

Regarding the practical method employed in the present project, two approaches can be mentioned regarding textual and archaeological material, respectively. For textual evidence, whether Egyptian or Chinese, the social status of the possible owner of the texts, whether inscribed on the tomb walls, written on papyrus or other material deposited in the tombs or elsewhere, needs to be considered to determine the social ramification of the texts in question. Excavated Chinese texts in particular should be studied against transmitted texts in order to determine their interpretive power. For example, the judgment as to whether a text found in a tomb should be used to illustrate a restricted local custom or more generally that of a wider area needs to be determined by examining evidence found in other places and in transmitted documents.

Archaeological material, including the tombs and funerary objects, need to be placed in a historical framework to determine their characteristics in the development of the funerary customs of respective cultures before they could be used as evidence in the discussion of the conceptualization of the netherworld in both Egypt and China. Similar to the textual evidence, whether one could employ a particular object as representing a local and temporal custom, or a more widespread and enduring custom, should be determined after judicious comparison with evidence found in other places dating from different time periods. It is important not to make generalizations easily, even within the same culture. Lastly, we need to exercise caution when drawing evidence from these two vastly different societies. We cannot overemphasize the need to pay constant attention to contexts and try avoiding over-generalization, anachronisms, or piecemeal comparison. The application of the aforementioned methodological concern will be demonstrated in the detailed research plan below.

## The Structure of This Book

After the introduction, Chapter 2 engages in a discussion of the evolution of tombs in Egypt and China. This chapter will utilize mainly archaeological material to reconstruct chronologically the archaeological expressions of the emergence of the idea of netherworld and its evolution over different eras, so as to obtain a basic understanding of the contours of the netherworld in ancient Egypt and China, in preparation for the next step of discussions.

The main point of this chapter is that the appearance of burials in human societies represents a collective imagination of certain kind of existence after death. Such imagination could be demonstrated by both the content and the physical structure of the tombs. This is because social customs were formed throughout history as collective consensus, and it should be legitimate for us to try to deduce the assumption behind the consensus and regard the funerary objects and tomb style as the outward expression of a collective imagination of the need of a person in the netherworld. The funerary ceremony that often performed before or after the burial, though also important for understanding the idea of the people concerning death and afterlife, was often not available in archaeological remains for the preliterate societies. For ancient Egypt and China, however, textual as well as iconographic evidence indeed could allow us some insight into the funerary rituals, which shall be discussed in the following chapters. Yet tomb styles that imitate the house of the living, found both in ancient Egypt and in China, speak volumes of an imagined residence in the netherworld.

Chapter 3 studies the iconographic representations of the netherworld, mainly using tomb paintings and funerary objects. The conceptual change underlying the development of tombs studied in Chapter 2 corresponded with the emergence of a more realistic imagination of a residence for the deceased. This was not merely an assumption based on the physical style of the tombs but could be demonstrated by the decorations in the tombs as well as the funerary objects. For example, the Opening of Mouth ritual, a ritual to enable the dead to use his/her mouth to speak and eat again, often depicted in New Kingdom Egyptian tombs and in the *Book of the Dead*, provides a vivid view of the need of the deceased to have certain physical function in the netherworld. The implication is that the imagination of life in the netherworld was intimately related to people's life experience.

Chapter 4 continues the pursuit of representations of the netherworld through mainly textual evidence. In addition to the pictorial evidence discussed in Chapter 3, religious texts provide important testimony for understanding the imagination of the netherworld. In ancient Egypt, the netherworld was described as consisting of a sequence of regions that the dead was supposed to pass through, and in each region there were different obstacles consisting of hostile deities and demons, intermixed with helpers and benevolent deities whose function was to make sure that the deceased will pass through the challenges and reach their destination. This destination was variously known as the Beautiful West, the Field of Offerings, or the Rosetau, the realm of Osiris, ruler of the netherworld. These will be analyzed against the social and natural environments of ancient Egypt.

As for the Chinese materials, in addition to tomb paintings, texts found in tombs reveal concerns with the life of the deceased in the netherworld, most likely based on their experience on earth. For example, texts found in tombs indicate that the world of the dead was ruled by a host of bureaucrats, and taxes and household registrations were practiced in this underground bureaucratic society. Such details of the netherworld seem to be more or less conditioned by this worldly experience.

A comparison between both visions of the netherworld and their relationship to life experience would enable us to gain further insight into the nature of each culture. This is to determine to what extent practical life experience could be seen as the factors that contributed to the imagination of the netherworld. It could be revealing to compare the life experience of different peoples and see if similar experiences would produce similar or different religious aspirations. Confucius once said, "Not yet understanding life, how could one understand death?." The original meaning of this sentence was supposedly to encourage the students to concentrate their attention on the tangible life on earth, rather than speculating on the intangible life after death. One could argue, however, that if we could comprehend how people imagined death, we can perhaps gain some new insight into their view of life.

Chapter 5 further explores the relationship between religious beliefs and social ethics, as well as how people imagined a life hereafter and its ethical foundation. Having obtained a graphic description of the netherworld in the last chapter, this chapter turns to the more abstract aspects of ethical values and social behavior that could have been the foundation of the visions of the netherworld. For example, in many Egyptian biographical inscriptions, there are some typical expressions that announce the virtue of the deceased: "I am son to the aged, father to the child, protector of the poor in every place. I have fed the hungry, anointed the unkempt, I have given clothing to the naked …." Such seemingly secular ethical values may have been the foundation of the belief in the judgment of the dead in later eras, as similar ethical principles appear in the form of negative confessions in the *Book of the Dead*.

On the Chinese side, although there was no systematic account of the netherworld, a number of texts found in tombs allude to certain social values, for example: "May the deceased in the tomb not be disturbed or have fear, and stay tranquil as before. It is decreed that the descendants shall increase in wealth and number, without misfortunes for thousands of years." Such social values are integral to the envisaging of a world after death.

Chapter 6 discusses the hope and fear of the Egyptian and the Chinese, and connects these themes to the search for happiness in both societies. While the hope for happiness is universal, the definition of happiness may differ from one culture to the next. This chapter will explore different genres of Egyptian texts such as the wisdom texts, biographies, letters, poems, as well as all the religious texts, to study the assumption behind these texts regarding an ideal state of existence or happiness. Similarly, Chinese texts and inscriptions discovered in the tombs are also employed to show how the fear of death and the hope for happiness were handled in Chinese society.

In the concluding chapter, we shall reflect upon the result of this effort to compare the idea of netherworld in these two ancient cultures. If the netherworld represented the paradise, as the Egyptians tended to assume, what mechanism was there to make this connection work? And what should or could this paradise consist of? As for the Chinese netherworld, what was the religious foundation, or the lack of it, that made it different from the Egyptian? This concluding chapter will therefore examine the ideas for and against the netherworld as a paradise and thus creates a more nuanced understanding of both societies and their religious beliefs.

Lastly, the driving force behind this study has been a desire to find a key to understand one aspect of humanity a little better. Everything that people in all societies ever wished to achieve could be summarized in one sentence—to seek for happiness, in various ways and expressions, with different understanding of what happiness is. This book purports to use a comparative method to analyze how this desire to achieve happiness was manifested in ancient Egypt and China, in particular their construction of the netherworld, by juxtaposing one against the other, to expose their similarities and differences, and to probe into the question of how to understand these similarities and differences, as a way to the understanding of humanity in general.[29]

---

[29] Translations of the original Chinese texts in this study, unless otherwise noted, are my own.

# 2

# The Evolution of Burial Style and the Imagination of the Netherworld

The appearance of burials in human societies, in whatever rudimentary fashion that people came up with, arguably marked a collective imagination of certain kind of existence after death. Regarding preliterate societies, it seems fair to assume that such ideas about afterlife could be recovered by analyzing the content of the funerary equipment. One could argue that the inclusion of funerary objects in the burial, no matter if they are only crude pots and pans, points to the belief in the existence of an idea of another form of life beyond death. That is to say, the deceased were given funerary objects because the living imagined that they would need these objects in their future lives. Alternatively, one could also argue that the inclusion of funerary objects might not necessarily be an indication of a conception of the netherworld, but simply an act of putting together and sending along what belonged to the deceased, to recognize the ownership of the objects. Such an argument could be found partially presented in the Confucian philosopher Xunzi's exposition of the meaning of funerary objects. Xunzi, in his writing, did not subscribe to the belief in the existence of the netherworld. For him, the funerary objects, whether real or surrogate, were meant to show respect for the deceased by treating the deceased as if they were still alive. The use of real objects once owned by the dead expressed a sentiment that the dead had not really gone. Yet since the living knew that the deceased would not be back to life, the objects were made incomplete in order to show the grief of the living. On the other hand, the inclusion of surrogate objects was clearly only for their spiritual value.[1] Even so, Xunzi could not deny that there was in his days a pervasive assumption that the dead were somehow able to possess or use the objects, thus implicitly pointed to a belief of another existence, however flimsily, in a netherworld.

---

[1] For discussion, see later and Mu-chou Poo (2011a).

In this study, we shall take the position to see the funerary objects as evidence for the existence of an idea of life after death. Whether the objects are real objects or surrogates and whether they imply different views of the netherworld would not affect this basic assumption. In so far as the funerary objects are produced within a certain social and historical context, representing a certain social grouping and social status or a certain belief system, part of the sociocultural system would inevitably be reproduced or transmitted through the objects and reveal to us certain aspects of the imagination of this other form of existence.

## The Evolution of Burial Style in Ancient Egypt

Given the abovementioned consideration, the prehistorical burials in Egypt, which usually consisted of a few potteries, seem to express an aspiration for a kind of future existence that needs water and sustenance, just like the need of the living.[2] As an Old Kingdom tomb inscription says,

> Oh you who live on earth, the *imakhu* (i.e. the blessed one) who love the god, and who shall pass by this tomb of mine of the necropolis, may you give bread, beer, and water from that which you possess! If you have none, then you shall speak with your mouths and offer with your hands: "a thousand of incense, a thousand of alabaster and clothing, oxen and fowl, oryxes and antelopes, [for so and so]" so you shall say.[3]

The inclusion of water jars in the burial, from a hindsight suggested by the abovementioned inscription, seems to be a silent testimony to the very humble desire of the deceased to gain a basic means for life, a sip of cold water in the parched desert. The text also clearly indicates that, for the deceased, an offering of prayer with imagined or visualized objects was just as good as real water, bread, and beer. They seemed to have already realized that the world of the dead was a place only in their imagination, and offerings, whether real, surrogate, or even only verbal, were equally effective. Indeed, an offering list was often inscribed on the wall of the tomb chamber, ensuring that the sustenance of the deceased should be provided.[4]

---

[2] Kathryn Bard (2012: 100).
[3] This is the so-called appeal to the living often found in Old Kingdom tombs; see an example in Strudwick (2005: 222). A classic study is Garnot (1938).
[4] Barta (1962); Morales (2015).

Another feature of the prehistorical burial is the direction of the head of the deceased. At several prehistorical cemeteries, the direction of the tomb was uniformly toward the west. At the Naqada I Amratian culture cemetery, for example, the deceased were in general placed in a contracted position and lying on the left side, with the head pointing to the south, but facing the west.[5] Since uniformity implies a certain collective social consensus, it becomes a challenge for us to discover what this consensus could have been. Suggestion has been made, based on the westward direction of the face, that there existed a belief in the West as the land of the dead, perhaps an early manifestation of the solar worship.[6] Given the abundant testimony of the belief in the West as the land of the dead in later Egyptian history, there is certain legitimacy for such a claim. Yet since not all the prehistorical burials have their direction toward the west, we should best not generalize the connection between the prehistorical burial custom and later beliefs.

The subsequent development of the pit burial into the mastaba at the end of prehistoric period and the beginning of the dynastic period indicated a further development of the imagination of the netherworld. The word "mastaba" originates from the Arabic language, which denotes a rectangular bench that ordinary households used. The earliest examples of mastaba are the tombs of the rulers of the so-called Dynasty 0 (*c.* 3300–2950 BCE) and the Early Dynastic period (First and Second Dynasties, *c.* 2950–2775 BCE) at Abydos and Saqqara, which usually consist of a number of chambers surrounding or next to the main burial chamber.[7] Judging by the remaining objects found in the chambers, they were mostly used as storages; thus, the entire structure suggests a residence with rooms of supplies, in spirit if not in actual architectural construction, indicating a more elaborate expression of the wish to have abundant sustenance in the netherworld. These royal tombs at Abydos are no doubt the manifestation of a long cumulative development of the conception of the afterlife. Moreover, evidence found in the subsidiary tombs indicates that the people buried there consisted of various professionals: in addition to those who served the king directly, there were artisans of wood, products, cloth, leather, or metal and stone, or persons who performed other administrative works. Thus the entire funerary compound, including the enclosure walls that could have served as ritual area, could be considered as a symbolic "world of the afterlife" that the deceased king

---

[5] Petrie and Quibell (1896); Shaw (2000: 47).
[6] Hoffman (1979: 110, 196).
[7] Dreyer (1988); O'Connor (2011).

**Figure 2.1** An idealized drawing of the mastaba. Old Kingdom.
*Source*: Drawing by T. H. Huang.

was expected to live in.[8] This basic setup arguably foreshadows the pyramid compound of the Third Dynasty and thereafter.

The mastabas of the First and the Second Dynasties were all built with mud bricks. Beginning from the Third Dynasty, however, a fundamental change was introduced in the building of the royal tombs, that is, building with stone. This change culminated with the completion of the funerary compound of King Zoser at Saqqara. This compound integrated the hitherto separated funerary structures such as the royal tomb, the subsidiary tombs and storages, the ritual space, and the funerary temple, and enclosed all within a rectangular wall, thus forming a comprehensive symbolic cosmos of the netherworld.[9]

It was also in the Third Dynasty that mastabas belonging to the noble individuals were constructed using stone material (Figure 2.1). During the subsequent dynasties, stone mastabas became a regular feature of the tombs of the nobles and officials. A typical mastaba usually consists of two parts: the aboveground and the underground. The underground part is a vertical shaft dug into the ground, with a horizontal burial chamber at the bottom that contains the coffin and funerary goods. Aboveground was a rectangular structure, consisting

---

[8] O'Connor (2011: 178–80).
[9] For an overview of this famous pyramid, see Lehner (1997).

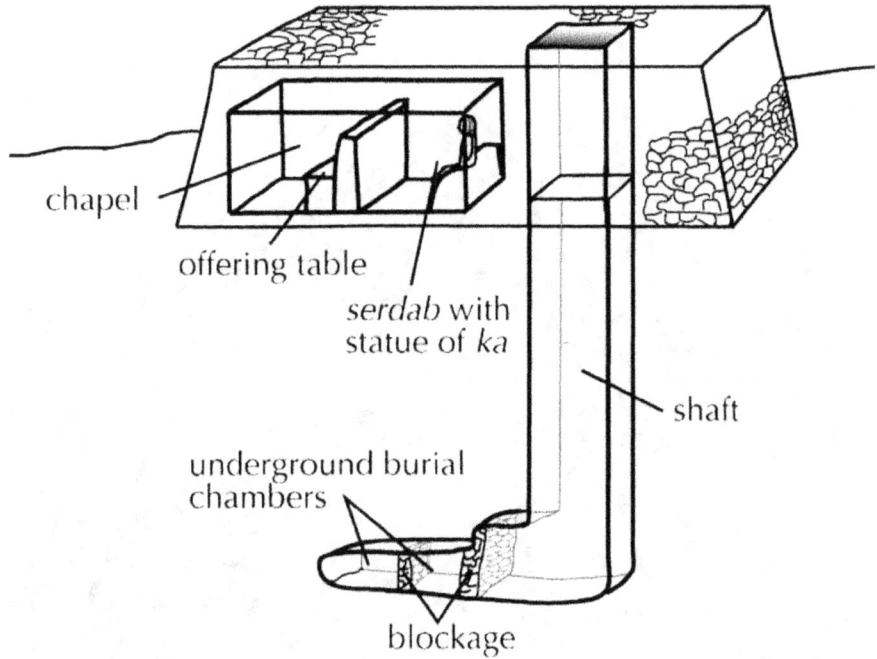

**Figure 2.2** A typical mastaba.
*Source*: Drawing by T. H. Huang.

of a chapel with an offering table. Often behind the offering table there is a false door with the statue of the deceased situated in the niche. Behind the false door, there is a room—called *serdab* in Arabic—containing the statue of the deceased.[10] The two parts of the aboveground structure may be interpreted as the living space of the deceased: the chapel is the living room, and the backroom is the chamber of repose.[11] (See Figure 2.2.)

This, however, does not mean that the older burial style disappeared completely. The vertical shaft tomb, for example, continues the pit tomb tradition since the prehistoric period. It can be said to be the precursor of the mastaba, since it is a shaft dug into the ground and has a side chamber at the bottom of the shaft to serve as the coffin chamber and storage. It is therefore the underground part of the typical mastaba, and the mastaba can be considered as the further development of this kind of shaft tombs. Such kinds of tombs were continued to be built in the Middle Kingdom period at Beni Hassan,[12] for example, long

---

[10] Bárta (1998: 65–75).
[11] For an archaeological summary, see Junker (1955). For a general account, see Kanawati (2001).
[12] See the report of the Middle Kingdom shaft tombs at Beni Hassan (Garstang 1907).

**Figure 2.3** Rock-cut tombs. Old Kingdom.
*Source*: Photo by author.

after the appearance of the mastaba, which reminds us that although burial customs change over time, the reality was much more complicated that cannot be summarized as a linear development. In this regard, it is also useful to note that the individual structure of each mastaba could vary greatly according to the social and political status of the owner.[13]

Beginning from the Old Kingdom, another burial style emerged as an alternative to mastaba. These are the rock-cut tombs (Figure 2.3). The earliest of this type of tombs are located at Giza and Saqqara, but most of them are found in Upper Egypt, in places such as the mountain slopes of Western Thebes, Aswan, Beni Hassan, and El-Hagarsa. During the Middle and New Kingdom periods, rock-cut tombs became the dominant tomb style for those who had the means to provide for themselves a tomb. Not only the kings of the New Kingdom built their rock-cut tombs in the valley to the West of Thebes, known as the King's Valley today, but the nobles and officials also built their tombs all over the hill side in Western Thebes.[14]

---

[13] Jánosi (2002).
[14] Poter and Moss (1960).

The basic feature of the rock-cut tomb was similar to that of the mastaba, with a front chapel composed of one or several rooms and an offering table with a false door behind it, a serdab (a small chamber) with the statue of the dead, and, if condition allows, storage rooms and a substructure consisting a shaft and burial chamber, similar to the setup in a typical mastaba. The difference, of course, is that the rock-cut tombs were excavated horizontally into a rock cliff, usually more elaborated than the mastaba and more costly in terms of construction.

The physical structure of the mastaba and the rock-cut tombs, moreover, created ample wall space that allowed the appearance of biographical texts, wall decorations, and the *ka*-statue in the tomb. They marked another important development in the Egyptian imagination of the netherworld. As the tomb served as the connection between the world of the living and the dead, any structural change to the tomb construction could potentially be a significant indication to a changed understanding of the tomb's function and therefore a changed understanding of the nature of the netherworld. This change, to be sure, was surely not a phenomenon that happened overnight, but a gradual, long-term evolution that might have escaped any living person's conscious notice. Thus the change can best be understood as a change in the collective mentality of the society.

Foremost among the changes are the appearance of the *ka*-statue and the painted or relief figures of the tomb owner and his/her family members featured on the door jambs and interior walls of the tomb. The figures and the accompanying scenes together formed a narrative about the life story of the tomb owner. At the same time, they expressed people's assumption about the relationship between the world of the living and that of the dead, as well as their belief or imagination of the netherworld. The tomb owner usually appears in the wall decoration to be attending various domestic activities or accepting offering items presented to him or her by family members or servants. We shall explore the meaning of these scenes and other graphic representations in the next chapter.

The appearance of the *ka*-statue of the deceased in the mastaba, such as the ones in the tomb of Mereruka[15] or Meresankh,[16] moreover, indicated in a concrete way the wish that the transformed soul of the deceased could walk out of the tomb and enter the daylight in another existence. The name of the

---

[15] Duell (1938).
[16] Dunham, Dows, and Simpson (1974).

funerary text that appeared in the New Kingdom and is known today as *Book of the Dead* actually has the title "Going forth by Day," which more accurately expresses the wish of the deceased as the *ka*-statue suggests.[17]

As we shall discuss the tomb paintings in Chapter 3, suffice it to say that, on balance, no matter how one should interpret these scenes of daily life in the Old Kingdom tombs, there is no doubt that they must have been a kind of representations of the actual life experience of the people then. One could see that the corresponding development in the area of technology and accumulated wealth might have contributed to the construction of the mastaba, but we should note that these were not the sufficient conditions for the building of the mastaba. The driving motivation for the construction of the mastaba, in the view of many, was probably the desire to build something to imitate the house of the living where the deceased could continue to live in an environment like that of the living people. The cemetery of mastabas at the Giza Plateau demonstrates this point well. These mastabas are lined up neatly as if they were the houses in a village along the streets, so that the relatives of the deceased could visit them just as they would visit a family or a friend's house.[18] (See Figure 2.1.)

This simple desire, that is, to imitate the house of the living, moreover, was probably not an isolated event but part of a development concomitant with many other features in the areas of religion, ethics, and cosmological speculations, not to mention economic capacity and technological progress. Evidence from the Old Kingdom onward shows that building a tomb also carried political implication, as it was a royal privilege to allow the nobles to build a tomb, often involving the king's permission or grant.[19] A typical formula often found on the door frames of the tombs has the following phrases:

> An offering that the king and Anubis at the fore of the god's booth have given, he having been given this tomb of his and burial in it, at the very end of old age, near the great god, lord of burial, (as) one *jm3ḫw* [i.e. venerated] with the king.[20]

Thus the development of the burial style and its corresponding change in the speculation of the netherworld marked not only the development of funerary custom, but also the changing collective mentality of society and culture in general. As M. Bárta puts it succinctly:

---

[17] Allen (1974).
[18] Allen (2006: 9–18). A good overview of the Giza cemetery can be found in Dunham (1974, plan A). An older classic is Reisner (1942).
[19] Alexanian (2006).
[20] Hassan (1960: 23 and pl. 8). Similar formula could be found in Sturdwick (2005: 209–16).

The spread of non-royal tombs cannot be assessed accurately if its context in society is neglected. This development was not uniformly linear: a sudden introduction of new elements into tomb architecture, or even the appearance of new tomb types, was always influenced by contemporary and prevalent social trends. During the reign of Nyuserra, tombs became very palpable indicators of social change and also accurately reflected contemporary social preferences. These underlying trends can be understood by looking at contemporary religious ideas and the economic as well as political situation, as reflected in the titles and status of individual officials and in their tomb decoration. We must then correlate the development of the tombs themselves with these very factors.[21]

Bárta was talking about the changes in the structure of mastaba during the Fifth Dynasty, and his focus was on some new elements in tomb structure that could reflect contemporary political, socioeconomic, or religious changes. What we are concerned here is the larger trend that might not be detected in one or two generations, but the underlying principle would not be much different from what Bárta had described.

The royal tombs and pyramids were always a special type of burial in terms of the extensiveness of the resources that were mustered to create a most distinguished monument to mark the supreme status of the king.[22] From the large royal tombs of the early dynasties to the pyramids of the kings of the Third to Sixth Dynasties, the intention of setting the royal tombs apart from the nonroyal tombs was clear. Yet whether this difference in the scale also implied a different view of the netherworld is a question that needs to be further investigated. By looking at the structure of the pyramid, with the connected funerary temple complex, one sees little resemblance with the mastaba or the rock-cut tombs of the nobles, which show more affinity with the idea of a residence that could accommodate the deceased. One could argue that the funerary temple was symbolic of the palace that the king lived in while on earth, as statues of the king were placed in the temple for the purpose of enjoying the offering rituals,[23] and the pyramids were after all evolved from the mastaba of the early dynastic period; thus, the royal netherworld would be the same as the nonroyal people except the scale of the residence. Whether such an argument could be sustained is an issue that needs to be discussed with the help of textual evidence such as the tomb inscriptions of the private persons and the *Pyramid Texts* that appeared in

---

[21] Bárta (2005).
[22] For a comprehensive introduction, see Lehner (1997).
[23] Arnold (1999).

the burial chambers of the pyramids since the Fifth Dynasty, which will be our subject in Chapter 4.

As for the royal tombs of the New Kingdom period, they were all rock-cut tombs that differ from the rock-cut tombs of the nobles since the Old Kingdom only in terms of the extensiveness of the tomb and the wall decorations. The so-called netherworld books that decorated the royal tombs demonstrated a special emphasis on some esoteric knowledge regarding the netherworld.[24] It remains to be seen, in Chapter 4, if and how this textual evidence could offer some more evidence regarding the royal afterlife.

## The Evolution of Burial Styles in Ancient China

With a long and continuous cultural development since the Neolithic period, the area of the East Asian subcontinent which was later known as China produced abundant archaeological as well as textual evidence for the development of its funerary culture. In the entire Neolithic period, however, various local traditions coexisted at the same time, and not until the beginning of the Shang Dynasty, when written documents appeared and when cultural cohesion strongly suggested that a mainstream cultural tradition was established in the area with Shang cultural dominance, could we talk more substantially about a funerary culture that was the hallmark of the Shang civilization.[25] For undeniably most of the Shang bronze artifacts now on display in various museums throughout the world came from tombs and were largely part of the funerary equipment. It was from the function, the style, the manufacturing technique, and the inscriptions on them that we learned various political, social, economic, and religious conditions of the Shang. Thus, the study of the funerary culture, of the tombs and their content, and of the ceremonies that accompanied the funeral may help us gain invaluable knowledge and insight into the Shang civilization, not the least the conception of the netherworld that people might have held. The same, of course, could be said of the later eras. With the increase of written documents, of course, the impact of funerary culture on our knowledge of the general cultural of a given period might have become less dominating. Nevertheless, the continuous development of funerary culture throughout ancient China until the end of the Han Dynasty

---

[24] Wilkinson (2016).
[25] Chang (1980).

makes a fascinating subject of study, as no written material alone could have provided.

The overwhelming majority of adult tombs from the Neolithic Yang-shao culture, the Mid-Yellow River Longshan culture, the Dawenkou culture, the Shandong Longshan culture, or even the Majiayao and Qijia cultures of the upper Yellow-River region were the so-called rectangular vertical pit.[26] This kind of tomb was basically a sunken rectangular pit dug directly into the ground. As for the means of burial, most of the tombs were earthen pits without coffin, and it was only in the Dawenkou culture that wooden coffins were found. Occasionally, the burial pit was lined with stones or pebbles, to isolate the body from the surrounding earth. Children were often buried in a large jar, as rarely also with some adults, which appear to be secondary burials. These anomalies notwithstanding, the general practice of body posture was the "extended face-up" posture, as opposed to "extended face-down" or "flexed" postures, which were less prevalent. One special feature was group burial. Already in the Yangshao period, same-sex group burials were found, and later in the Dawenkou and Majiayao cultures there were couple burials, indicating certain change in the social structure and perhaps the rise of the nuclear family. Another important aspect was the appearance of certain ritual objects in the burials, including jade axe and other ceremonial objects such as *cong* (琮) and *yazhang* (牙璋), as well as thin clay containers. Other funerary objects usually consisted of utensils used in day-to-day lives such as clay pots, bone needles, stone pebbles, ear rings, tools, and so on.[27] Thus one could say that by the end of the Neolithic period, burials along the Yellow River basin had acquired some features that constitute the basic elements of the burial customs of the Shang Dynasty and later eras—vertical pit wooden casket tomb, extended face-up burial posture, and ritual objects that could indicate the social and political statuses of the deceased.

Like the Egyptian case, when society developed into a more complicated and stratified structure, the powerful and the rich would tend to bury their dead in a more elaborate fashion, to show their social distinction. Lager tombs, more funerary objects, lavish coffins, and caskets were expectedly what would be found with the burials of the ruling class. The Shang Dynasty, apparently due to the accumulation of resources and concentration of power resulting from many generations of development, was able to deploy the resources to develop a funerary culture that echoed the growing power of the royalty. The astounding

---

[26] See Poo (1993, chapter 1).
[27] Poo (1993, chapter 1).

royal tombs excavated at the site of Yinxu 殷墟, the present city of Anyang, Henan Province, together with thousands of small tombs and some mid-size tombs that might have belonged to the commoners and nobles, respectively, give us a good overview of the funerary culture of the Shang.[28]

The clear contrast between the sizes of the tombs indicates the formation of a hierarchical society divided into the rulers, the nobles, the commoners, and the slaves. A study of the tombs of this period shows that, at Yinxu, a good indication of the status of the tomb owner was not only the size of the tomb, but also the ramps leading to the tomb pit, obviously for construction purpose. The larger the tomb, the more ramps were needed. Take tomb no. 1001 for example; its top dimension measures 18.9 m × 13.75 m, and bottom floor dimension measures 16 m × 11 m, with a depth of 10.5 m, and with four ramps on each side of the burial pit. The longest ramp measures 30.7 m × 7.8 m; the shortest measures 7.4 m × 3.75 m.[29] Altogether archaeologists found seventeen large tombs, among which eight were with four ramps, eight were with two ramps, and one was with one ramp. Whether all these were tombs of the kings or whether those with one or two ramps were persons of a lesser status is of course not easy to determine without written evidence.[30] One could at least point out that the tomb of the queen of King Wu Ding (c. 1250–1192 BCE), Fu Hao, did not have any ramp, though her tomb contained abundant funerary objects when it was found.[31]

From the findings in the tomb of Fu Hao, we gain the impression that the burial process was a rather lengthy and complicated one. At an early stage of the burial, sacrificial pits for animals (mainly dogs) and people were dug at the bottom of the burial pit. Wooden caskets would then be constructed in the center of the burial pit. When the casket was completed and the coffin and funerary objects were placed in the casket, the earth was filled in. At different levels of this filling in, sacrificial victims—humans or dogs—were placed, some on top of the casket and some to the side. Other funerary objects were also buried at different depths of the burial pit, suggesting that certain rituals took place at the moment of interment.[32] Based on this, one could surmise that in the larger tombs of the kings, with many more human sacrificial victims and certainly more funerary objects, the burial process would involve even more elaborate rituals.

[28] Chang (1980: 110–24); Poo (1993, chapter 1).
[29] Liang and Gao (1963: 17).
[30] Poo (1993, chapter 1).
[31] Zhongguo shehui kexueyuan (1980).
[32] Zhongguo shehui kexueyuan (1980: 7–12).

The most extraordinary aspect of the Shang Royal burial, to our modern eye at least, was the custom of human sacrifice. Without going into the details, suffice it to say that it was the custom of the day that the Shang king took with him many people, voluntarily or not, to the netherworld. To take the example of tomb no. 1001, archaeologists found more than 164 victims scattered in various locations in the tomb.[33] Some of these were provided with coffins and funerary objects, and some were without such equipment. A large number of them were beheaded and lay in rows on the ramps, among which were children and young adolescents.[34] Thus we can see that the sacrificial victims also consisted of different statuses: those who were close to the king, such as retinues or guards, and those who were mere servants, workers, or even slaves. In the tomb of Fu Hao, for another example, at least sixteen people were sacrificed to accompany the queen.[35] Apparently, the custom of human sacrifice was quite prevailing at this time, as more than 200 mass graves for human sacrifice were found at the site of Anyang, with more than 1,300 bodies inside.[36]

The practice of human sacrifice at funerals lasted throughout the Shang and in the subsequent Western Zhou and down to the Eastern Zhou and the Warring States period.[37] Although the practice was probably not as prominent as the Shang period and less people were sacrificed, the fact that such a kind of practice could last for such a long time, despite certain protests from the more conscious intellectuals in the society, indicates a strong conservative element in the funerary custom among the ruling class. This long tradition of vertical pit burial style, exemplified by the late Shang royal tombs at Anyang, demonstrates a stable cultural practice that was closely related to the idea of the netherworld.

What was notable was that the ancient Chinese developed out of this burial style a system that was designed to reflect the political and social status of the deceased. This system was much more than simply to show off the wealth of the deceased by piling whatever objects, real or surrogate, that one could afford. Using several classical texts, we can reconstruct this system as it was practiced during the pre-Qin period (eighth to third century BCE) as the following:[38] when the king dies, his burial would consist of seven layers of coffins and caskets; for a prince, the burial would consist of five layers of coffins and caskets; for an official, it would consist of three layers of coffins and caskets; and for a

---

[33] Liang and Gao (1963: 17).
[34] Liang and Gao (1963: 17).
[35] Zhongguo shehui kexueyuan (1980: 8–19).
[36] Chang (1980: 123–4).
[37] Huang (1990).
[38] For the following discussion on burial styles, see Poo (1993, chapter 2).

gentleman, it would consist of two layers of coffins and caskets. In accordance with the number of the coffins and caskets, the deceased would be supplied with a certain number of funerary objects, most prominent among them bronze vessels such as *ding, gui, hu, he,* and so on. For the king, therefore, nine *ding*s and eight *gui*s would be supplied; for the prince, seven *ding*s and six *gui*s would be supplied; for the officials, five *ding*s and four *gui*s would be supplied; and for the gentleman, three *ding*s and two *gui*s would be supplied. Similarly, the shape of the burial pit would also conform to a hierarchical order: the tomb of the king would consist of four ramps; that of the prince would consist of two ramps; that of the high ranking noble would consist of one ramp; and the gentleman would have no ramp at all.

Since this seemingly logical and hierarchical system was a reconstruction, first by the redactors of the classical texts and then by modern scholars, there may be some doubt as to whether it had ever existed as a universal institution at any given point in history. Archaeological findings in the pre-Qin period, however, indicate that indeed in a certain period and at a certain area the funerary establishment conformed to a hierarchical order, presumably the result of a long period of evolution, reflecting the politico-social status of the deceased. Thus, it is reasonable to assume that this system represented a general consensus among the ruling class regarding burial practices at least till the end of the Spring and Autumn periods. From the Warring States period onward, because of the disintegration of the Zhou feudal system, the number of coffins and bronze vessels gradually lost their value as indicators of the deceased's social and political status. This was probably not because people's idea about the symbolic meanings of the number of coffins and bronze vessels had changed. On the contrary, it was likely because of too many upstarts of this chaotic period were anxious to join the ranks of the old nobility by appropriating funerary equipment that exceeded their original sociopolitical status that the differentiating force of the system began to fade. However, this self-aggrandizing tendency still recognized coffins and funerary objects as symbols of wealth, which is not incompatible with the deceased's political status. Concurrent with this is the increase in the amount and variety of objects of daily use, surrogate or real, that are found in the tombs. The meaning of this tendency is to be considered together with the change of tomb style just below.

When time moved into the Han period, the old coffin and casket system fell even more into the background. The burial of Lady Dai, wife of Marquis Dai, who died around 168 BCE, consists of six layers of coffins and caskets, which exceeded what was usually prescribed for a person of her status, that is, five layers

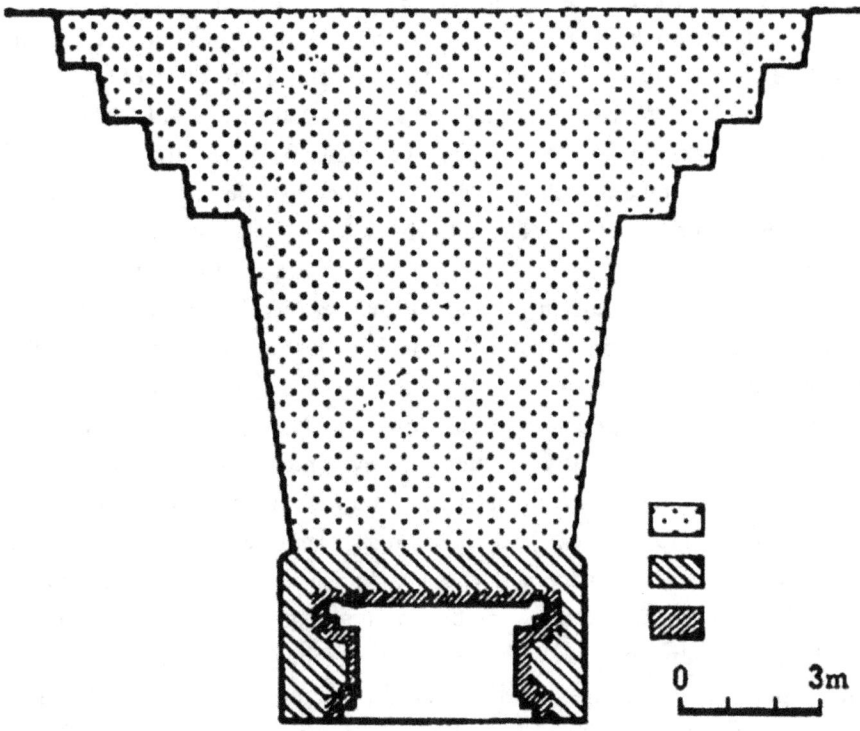

**Figure 2.4** Idealized line-drawing of a vertical-pit wooden-casket tomb.
*Source*: Drawing by T. H. Huang. After Hunan sheng bowuguan and Zhongguo kexueyuan kaogu yanjiusuo (1973, vol. 1, fig. 3).

if we still employ the old system. On the other hand, her husband, the Marquis Dai, possessed only four layers of coffins and caskets, which was a degree below that of his wife if the number of coffins still has any status-symbolic meaning.[39] It is remarkable that even in the same family the burial of the wife could be more elaborated than the husband. How to explain this discrepancy, however, remains unresolved. Moreover, archaeological discoveries of early Han dynasty tombs indicate that at this time there was no strictly followed burial practice that corresponded to political status in an exact way.[40] Individual differences or preferences certainly played a more significant role than before.

A few Western Han tombs that belonged to feudal kings and nobilities displayed a particular burial style. It was basically a wooden casket tomb (Figure 2.4) at the

---

[39] Hunan sheng bowuguan and Zhongguo kexueyuan kaogu yanjiusuo (1973); Hunan sheng bowuguan and Hunan sheng wenwu gaogu yanjiusuo (2004).
[40] Poo (1993: 62–8).

center, yet the outer casket was built in an extensive way that included a corridor surrounding the inner chamber and an anti-chamber with two doors. The entire structure thus resembles a wooden house. Still outside, a thick wall of wood piles surrounded the casket-burial chamber, forming a protective shield. The Chinese term for this style is *huangchang ticou* (黃腸題湊). Alternatively, the entire structure would be built with stone blocks, which was perhaps a compromise between the wooden casket tomb and the brick tomb.[41] The tomb of the deposed emperor Liu He 劉賀 (92–59 BCE), known as the marquis of Hai Hun (海昏侯), excavated in 2011 in Nanchang, Jiangxi Province, reveals a structure basically similar to the Mawangdui tombs, but with a narrow corridor surrounding the wooden casket chambers and thus could be regarded as belonging to the *huangchang ticou* style, perhaps an example of an early stage of the development.[42]

Some other kings' tombs were built in an even more expensive way. A good example is the tomb of the king of Zhongshan, Liu Sheng, who was the cousin of Emperor Jing (156–140 BCE), therefore slightly later than Lady Dai. His rock-cut tomb, situated in Mancheng, Hebei Province, was in the shape of a double cross, that is, two pairs of side chambers built along a 51.7-meter-long central axis.[43] The side chambers, as with many brick tombs of similar structure, were each supplied with carriages, kitchen utensils, and food. Inside the main burial chamber, a wooden house was built, thus creating a practical residence for the deceased. Notably, even with his status as a king, Liu Sheng had only one coffin and one casket, corroborating our observation that the old rule of using five layers of coffins and caskets for the king was not followed. In any case, with such structures, there should be no doubt that the tombs were now meant to be the house of the deceased in a realistic sense. Rock-cut cave tombs such as Liu Sheng's tomb were of course only affordable by the most powerful kings.[44]

A number of rock-cut tombs (Figure 2.5) with long corridors and side chambers were also found in the Xuzhou area, Jiangsu Province, also dated to the Western Han period and belonged to the kings of the vassal state of Chu. One large tomb measures about 55 meters deep into the rock, with eighteen chambers of various sizes.[45] If one looks at the plan of these tombs, one cannot but be amazed of how these tombs look like the royal tombs of the Egyptian New Kingdom pharaohs at the Valley of the Kings in Western

[41] Poo (1993: 62–8); Huang (2003: 75–82).
[42] Wang and Wang (2016).
[43] Zhongguo shehui kexue kaogu yanjiusuo and Hebeisheng wenwu guanlichu (1980).
[44] See Huang (2003: 82–7).
[45] Qiu (1988). See Poo (1993: 67–8).

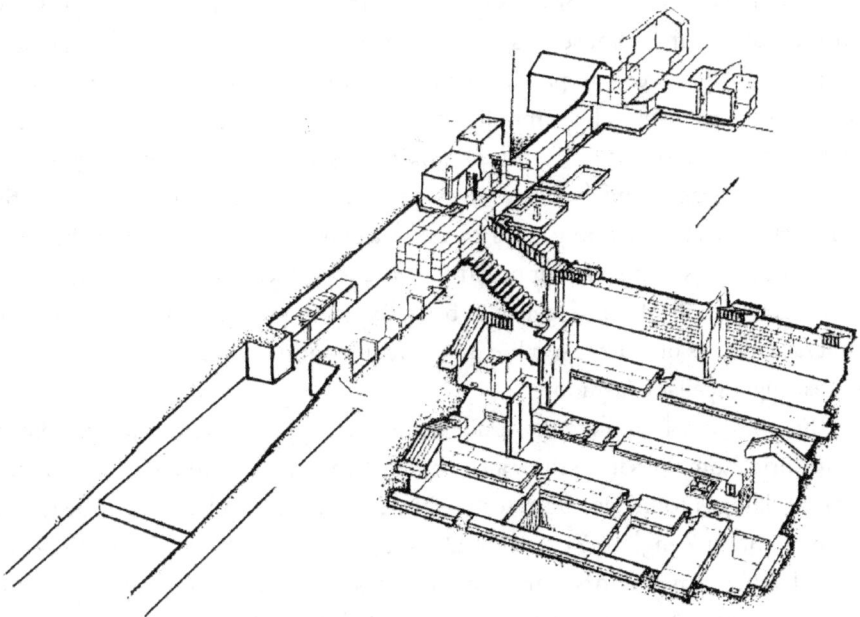

**Figure 2.5** A rock-cut tomb at Beidongshan, Western Han period. Jiangsu.
*Source*: Drawing by T. H. Huang. After Qiu Yongsheng (1988).

Thebes.[46] Apparently there were similar urges in both China and Egypt to dig deep into the rock as far as possible, as such a magnificent scale would enhance the appearance of regal status.

It was also in the Han period that another significant change in funerary practice occurred. This is the appearance of horizontal brick tombs. In its earlier form, the tomb was constructed by large bricks that replaced the wooden outer casket of the vertical pit tomb. This kind of tomb first appeared in the late Warring States period, although the exact reason why they appeared remains conjectural.[47] Without going into a detailed discussion, the fact is that during the early Western Han period, this burial style gradually gained acceptance, and the structure of the tomb also began to develop into more complicated forms. Now the brick burial chamber grew larger, often with an anti-chamber, some even with two side chambers serving as storage for funerary objects. It was therefore more like an underground house for the deceased. This tendency to imitate the house of the living was even more obvious when decorative wall paintings and

[46] Poo (1993: 68–72).
[47] Huang (2003: 41–2, 90–5). See also Lai (2015, chapter 2).

reliefs were added to the brick wall, similar to those that people used to hang on the walls in their houses, as we know from written documents.[48] The side chambers, if they were supplied, were often divided according to the functions they served: one would be symbolic of a kitchen and therefore kitchen utensils and foodstuffs were stored; another would be symbolic of the carriage house and thus carriages and horses were supplied. These, of course, were mostly surrogate objects, including figurines of various types, representing different sorts of servants that were supposed to serve the deceased in the world below. It seems that, with the emergence of brick tombs (Figure 2.6) and the supply of funerary objects of daily use, a life in the netherworld had been conceived in an increasingly realistic fashion.

This tendency to imitate the residence of the living was not only represented by the brick tombs. Within the tradition of the vertical pit wooden casket tombs, similar changes could also be detected. The earliest sign of change may be found in the tomb of Zenghou Yi (c. 477–433 BCE), dated to the early Warring States period, where small doors were constructed on the walls of the caskets so that different burial chambers were connected. Although the doors might only be symbolic and without any practical function, the meaning seems clear: the souls of the deceased were expected to move around in the tombs through the doors, much like what they used to do in the houses when alive.[49] Thus it could be seen as an explicit reference to the idea that the tomb was conceived as a house for the deceased. During the late Warring States and early Western Han periods, in the area of the old Chu state, some wooden casket tombs were developed into a kind of two-story structure, with features of doors, windows, and stairs that connected the upper and lower levels. Several of them even had pigpens in the lower level, which undoubtedly were imitations of the house of the living. Funerary objects such as clay models of rice paddies, boats, carriages, cattle, chicken, and fish only further confirm this intention.[50] Thus one can say that there was an inner change in the traditional vertical pit tomb: the overall burial style remains the same, but the structures of the caskets began to show references to the house of the living.

What is becoming obvious by now is that, whether in the traditional vertical pit wooden casket tombs or the newly developed brick tombs, rock-cut tombs, or the luxurious tombs, a new trend became prevalent during the early Western Han period. This was an increasing tendency to imitate the

---

[48] Xing (1986).
[49] Hubeisheng bowuguan (1989).
[50] For the following, see Poo (1993: 121, 196–7); Huang (2003: 61–9).

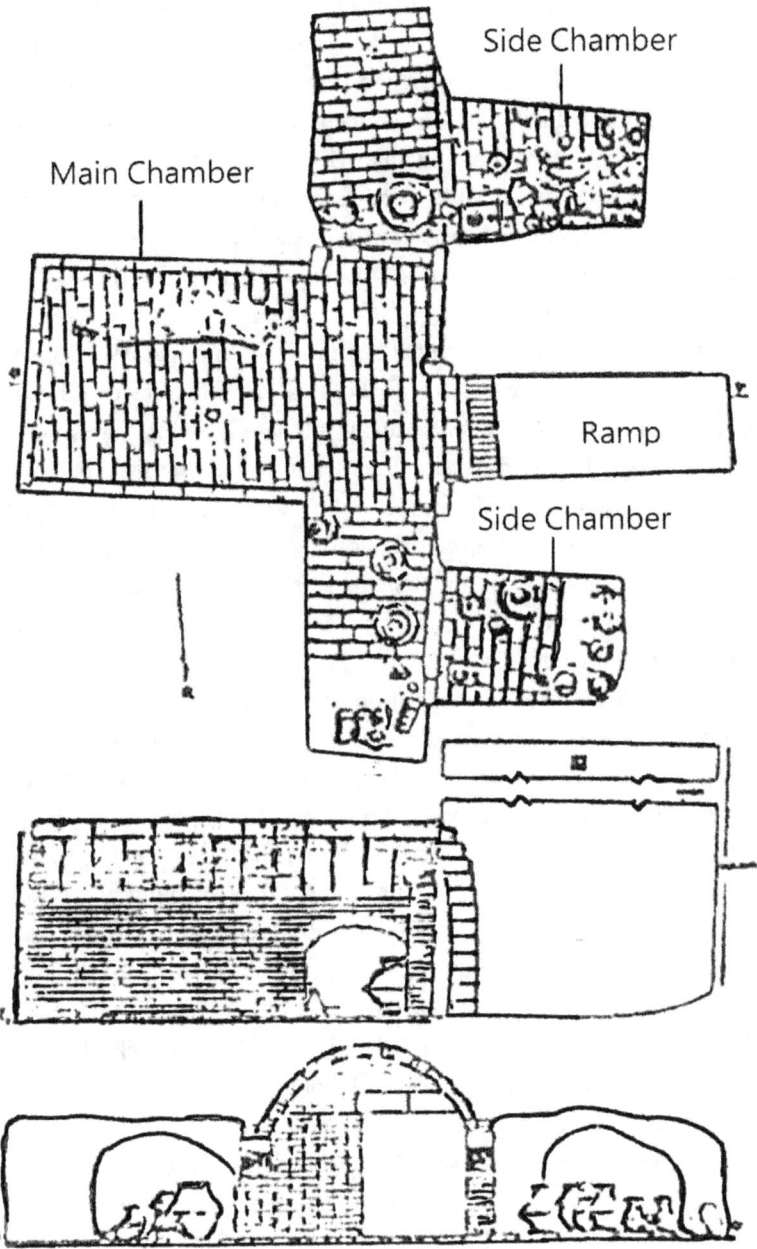

**Figure 2.6** A typical brick tomb. Eastern Han.
*Source*: Drawing by T. H. Huang. After Zhongguo kexueyuan kaogu yanjiusuo (1959: 25, fig. 11, no. 82).

house of the living. It is significant because burial customs are usually some of the most important social conventions, and changes in such conventions would certainly have represented a corresponding change in people's mentality concerning life and death or even conceptions of life after death. It seems that the trend was toward creating an environment for the deceased that was similar to that of the living. This implies that people began to imagine, in a more realistic way, that the deceased would lead a life after death like the one on earth. A question could be raised immediately: how did the change come about, and why at this time?

As with the case of early Egypt, the remains of prehistorical grave goods demonstrate the possible existence of the idea of a life after death. Therefore we cannot assume that it was only during the late Warring States period that the Chinese people began to develop the idea of a netherworld. The problem is, why, in building their tombs, did people not try to imitate the house of the living until this time? Or one may even ask, could we regard the vertical pit tombs of the Shang Dynasty with compartments as already showing the intention of imitating the house of the living? Short of a definite explanation, we can only try to find the answer in the social and political changes that ensued during the Warring States—Qin–Han transition. It has been mentioned that, due to the change in the socioeconomic structure of the Spring and Autumn periods, many formerly lower-class people had risen on the social ladder. One way to mark their success was to adopt the burial custom of the upper class, which was formerly denied of them.[51] Further, because of the growing trend of the establishment of centralized and bureaucratic governments, the traditional feudal values based on class and clan were gradually replaced by a new value system that esteemed individual achievement rather than clan background. The result of this sociopolitical change was also reflected in the fact that burial objects representing wealth and comfort in daily life, including surrogate houses, wells, cattle, and fields, gradually superseded, though perhaps did not completely replace, the old emphasis on political status represented by the hierarchical system of coffins and bronze vessels. The construction of tombs that imitate the living quarters on earth, therefore, would be part of this emphasis on a material representation of a new social consciousness. As I tried to argue elsewhere, this emphasis on postmortem personal wealth and comfort could only have been realized in a society that allowed and even encouraged personal achievement.[52]

---

[51] Poo (1998: 165–7).
[52] Poo (1998:176–7). See also Lai (2015, chapter 2).

The Warring States—Qin–Han transition period, when the old clan-based class society gradually crumbled, seems to be an ideal breeding ground for this new trend in funerary custom.

## Comparative Note

When we compare the Egyptian tombs with the Chinese tombs, it should be remembered that tombs were not created outside of the geographic and physical environment. It is easy to see that the Egyptian landscape was dominated by the Nile and the narrow alluvial plain along the river, flanked by the desert on both sides. Since tombs were built outside of the cultivation area, builders of the Egyptian tombs had to deal with basically sand and rock. Whereas in China, because of the variety of landscape, tombs could be built in the loess plateau, in the central plain, along the Yangtze valley, and in the mountainous areas, with many local variations.[53]

Returning to the Egyptian case, except for the great royal tombs of the Early Dynasty period, most burials before the rise of the mastaba are shallow pit tombs, which bespoke a rather intuitive and widely practiced burial practice, and were also in line with the general material condition in Egypt. George A. Reisner had long ago already laid out the general trend of the development of Egyptian tombs in early Old Kingdom.[54] At the beginning, it was a vertical pit tomb, low tech, low cost, and easy to make. When wealth accumulated and technology developed came the mastabas, which were basically expensive vertical pit tombs, lined sometimes with wooden caskets or bricks, with subsequent elaboration of aboveground structure that constituted of offering chamber and the serdab that enabled ritual activities to be performed in the chamber. This change from the vertical pit to the vertical-plus-horizontal construction, which is more difficult to make, could be interpreted as imitation of the house of the living. It is conceivable, therefore, that there was, similar to the Chinese case, also a corresponding development in people's perception or visualization of a possible next life, in an abode wherein the dead were supposed to spend their time happily ever after, that is, the house of eternity (*pr n nḥḥ*).

Our survey of the development of tombs shows that there was a change in people's attitude toward imagining a more comfortable afterlife that bore

---
[53] See Poo (1993, chapters 2, 3).
[54] Reisner (1942).

resemblance to the life of the living. Building the tomb to imitate or to symbolize the house of the living could be one effort within the trend of change to foster this imagination. This may sound very attractive and seemingly logical, but there is still the gap between interpreting the meaning of the change in funerary architecture and identifying hard evidence to substantiate the reason for the change. We are not quite sure which came first: the change in the tomb style or the need for a comfortable abode for life after death? One possibility, while a little obvious to suggest, would be that the development from pit tomb to mastaba in Egypt was concomitant with the rise of the state power and social wealth in the Third Dynasty; thus, the mastaba represented a stage of economic prosperity that allowed a sector of the elite to build such tombs. The rise of the vertical pit wooden casket tomb in China in the Shang Dynasty also corresponded with the accumulation of wealth in society, represented by the rise of bronze industry. Thus both in Egypt and in China, the changing burial style corresponded to, if not dependent upon, the changing material condition of the society. That is to say, the changing imagination of the netherworld or conception of life after death was not merely a social sentiment developed out of nothing; there had to be a good measure of material condition that allowed any imagination to develop and to be realized. Since both the Egyptian mastabas and rock-cut tombs and the Chinese brick tombs of the Han Dynasty carry abundant pictographic as well as textual sources, not to mention the rich funerary objects, an investigation into these sources could provide us with more clues to our questions regarding the imagination of the netherworld.

One important difference between China and Egypt was the extent to which the king had the control of granting a tomb to the nonroyal people. A standard formula "An Offering which the king gives and which Anubis who dwells in the divine tent-shrine gives that he may be buried in the necropolis," which can be found in almost every inscribed tomb in Egypt, speaks emphatically how the private tombs were tightly connected to the authority of the king. Even in a relatively small tomb, such as the Sixth Dynasty tomb of Tetiseneb in Saqqara, the following words were inscribed: "Regarding this tomb which I made in the necropolis, the king it was who gave me its location as I was/so that I might be an *imakhu* (revered spirit) in the sight of the king, for I always do what his lord favors."[55]

In China, the closest textual indication of the granting of royal patronage was probably the stipulation regarding the layers of coffins and caskets used and the

---

[55] Sturdwick (2005, no. 189). Many similar statements can be found throughout the Old Kingdom.

number of bronze vessels provided for the burials.⁵⁶ Yet these were found not in the tombs but in the classical texts such as the *Book of Rites* (*Liji*), which was not a royal document, and there is no clear indication about whether the king should as a rule provide the burials and funerary objects for his subjects or oversee whether any funerary setup exceeded or "usurped" the proper paraphernalia according to the status of the deceased. Many of the Shang and Zhou bronze vessels bear inscriptions that identify the maker of the vessels, and many of them were made by the deceased or his/her family members, not the king. This may at least hint at the fact that the nobles had the freedom to assemble their own funerary equipment. In any case, if the king had certain control of the burials of his subjects, it was not obvious from the burials and funerary objects, except that he would be the one who controls wealth and technology in general. The supposedly hierarchical funerary system described earlier fell into disarray at least since the Warring States period, as the Zhou Dynasty royal power declined with the rise of powerful local kingdoms, and thereafter, the burial of individuals, whether royal or private, was contingent mostly on the wealth of the deceased, which can be said to be a new system based on wealth and power that did not necessarily comply with a person's political status or relationship with the ruler. This is not only our modern interpretation of the archaeological material. An Eastern Han scholar named Zhao Zi (fl. mid-second *c*. CE) once gave a very succinct description of the evolution of burial customs prior to his time:

> The *Yijing* says: the ancient people buried the dead with tree branches and hid the corpse in the middle of the wilderness. The saints of later era changed this custom by introducing the use of coffins and caskets. The making of coffins and caskets began from the Yellow Emperor, followed by Emperor Yao, down to the Xia Dynasty. At the time people still prefer simplicity, using either clay or wood [for the coffin]. When it came to the Shang Dynasty the burial became more elaborate, and the Zhou Dynasty followed the Shang custom. They used multiple layers of coffins with decorations and banners to identify the dead. They performed rituals to recall the soul and put jade in the mouth of the dead. They divined for the date of burial, and observed the system of layers of the coffins and caskets, with the set number of clothes to dress the dead. These measures were numerous and of no practical effect, and the materials needed were many and hard to prepare. Yet the hierarchical order was set to distinguish the noble and the commoners. From King Cheng (c. 1042–1006 BCE) and King Kang (c. 1005–978 BCE) onward, the system began to decline a little. When it came

⁵⁶ *Liji zhengyi* (1976, juan 28, p. 22). See detailed discussion in Poo (1993: 25–7); Poo (1990).

to the Warring States period, the system was mostly destroyed and rules and regulations were abandoned, people of lower status usurped the privileges of the higher class. Thus the Duke Wen of Jin asked to build his tomb with a ramp [which was the privilege of the Zhou king], the Duke Mu of Qin used human sacrifice for his tomb, an official of Chen built three layers of casket [which was over what his status deserved], and the minister Huan of Song built a luxurious stone casket for himself.[57]

Zhao Zi's observation is surprisingly close to what modern archaeologists could have suggested. It is certain that Zhao Zi was not an archaeologist, and all his knowledge about the history of the burial customs came from either his learning from ancient texts such as the *Commentary of Zuo* (*Zuozhuan* 左傳) or from oral traditions. Here we detect another difference between Egypt and China: the Egyptians never seemed to have any doubt about the legitimacy of their burial customs, whereas the Chinese intellectuals, beginning from Confucius, down to the Han Dynasty literati and beyond, had for a long time debated about what a proper burial should be, what will happen when a person is dead, and therefore what was the use and meaning of funerary objects, whether real or surrogate.[58] Of course there were also voices in ancient Egypt that expressed a disillusion or skepticism about whether the tomb could last forever, yet these were remorse about the brevity of life, not about the fundamental meaning of life. All these Chinese sources constitute an interesting contrast with the Egyptian material, which we shall continue to explore in the following chapters.

---

[57] *Houhanshu* (1965; 39: 1314–15).
[58] Poo (1990).

3

# Iconographic Representations of the Netherworld

It is a fact of humanity that human imagination, despite its capacity to create new things that had not existed before, relies heavily on previous experience that the mind had absorbed during its life course. Arguably, all human creations are built on previous knowledge and accumulated imagination in one way or another, and in different combinations and syntheses. Our analysis of the ideas of the netherworld in ancient Egypt and China will therefore be based on this understanding. Since no one has returned from the netherworld, either in Egypt or in China, all the descriptions of the netherworld, either visual or textual, are necessarily constructed based on the life experience of the people in these societies.

As discussed in Chapter 2, the conceptual change underlying the development of tombs corresponded with the emergence of a more realistic imagination of a residence for the deceased. This was not merely an assumption based on the physical style of the tombs. It could be borne out by graphic and textual evidence. In the case of Egypt and China, the evidence came from tomb paintings, funerary objects, as well as various texts either inscribed in the tombs, preserved on papyrus rolls, or preserved on bamboo slips that contain reference to the netherworld. This chapter shall discuss mainly graphic evidence from the tombs.

## Graphic Representations in Egyptian Tombs

Beginning from the Third Dynasty when stone mastabas were built, decoration with texts, paintings, and reliefs were a regular feature. For the modern spectators, the paintings and reliefs provided a direct testimony to the life and belief of the Egyptians. The scenes of daily life have long been regarded as representing an idealized expression of a prosperous household of the deceased. The question is, are these scenes representations of the tomb owner's expected future life in the netherworld, or are they reminiscence of the deceased's past life, to commemorate and celebrate his/her time on earth?

Arguments for the first position, that is, the scenes depict an ideal future life that the deceased would enjoy in the netherworld, see the paintings as having the function of funerary objects, and by depicting scenes of happy daily life they could somehow have the magical effect to allow the deceased to lead the kind of life depicted. It is known that the custom of spell casting was common in Egyptian society. The pictures, by analogy, were the equivalent of the spells, and by depicting some scenes, they were expected to come into being to be enjoyed by the dead. Indeed, the famous Egyptologist W. C. Hayes once made the following observation:

> Relief sculpture and painting appeared in mastaba tombs at the end of the Third Dynasty. The first part of the tomb so decorated was the rectangular lintel over the false-door stela, whereon the deceased is shown seated before the funerary repast. Subsequently the chapel walls were decorated with a panorama of the dead man's earthly possessions and of his servants producing everything essential to his welfare, *in the belief that these presentments of reality were endowed with the essence of the originals and would supply him with his needs for all time*. The stela is usually inscribed with appropriate offering formulae and with the name and titles of the owner of the tomb. Large figures of the deceased and of members of his family occur on salient architectural elements, such as the jambs of the entrance doorway of the chapel, the lateral panels of the stela, and the jambs and reveals of the stela niche.[1]

Hayes's position reflects a general assumption of the meaning of the tomb paintings. According to this assumption, the paintings depict the daily life of the deceased and his/her funeral, which was the last impression that the deceased could have made to the world and his/her descendants. At the same time, these scenes were done "in the belief that these presentments of reality were endowed with the essence of the originals and would supply him [the deceased] with his needs for all times." If we accept this position, then there is a reason to say that the Egyptians believed that life in the netherworld would be like what the deceased had experienced on earth. This view could very well be true, especially with the support of other textual evidence that we shall discuss later. However,

---

[1] Hayes (1946).

there is no direct indication in the tomb paintings in the Old Kingdom and Middle Kingdom periods that suggest that the scenes represented life in the netherworld. It was only in the New Kingdom that some tombs were decorated with the scenes from the *Book of the Dead*, especially Spell 110 showing the Field of Offerings, which depicts a netherworld scenario. The decorations in the New Kingdom royal tombs depicting books of the netherworld, such as the Amduat or the *Book of the Gate*, however, are strictly a royal privilege in the New Kingdom.[2] Further investigation is therefore needed to reach a more satisfactory understanding.

In the Egyptian tombs, whether the mastabas or rock-cut tombs, besides the images of the deceased on the door frames and the false door, which serve to identify the owner of the tomb, the various paintings in the tombs could roughly be divided into two broad categories. There are first of all funerary scenes, including the funeral processions of offering bearers and wailing women, and offering table scenes where the deceased were receiving food offerings, sometimes with the persons making the offerings in an opposite position to the deceased. While it is unnecessary to go over every scene in every tomb to ascertain that these funerary scenes were representations of real events, there is little reason to doubt that the scenes carried a high degree of individual characteristics and specific features that pertain only to the deceased tomb owner. In the tomb of Mereruka (Figure 3.1), for example, every mortuary priest in the ceremonial procession was presented with personal names,[3] and in a scene that shows Mereruka sitting on a chair, with his wife sitting in front and his brothers and sons standing behind him, inspecting the presentation of offerings by the mortuary priests, the individual names of his brothers and sons were all given in the painting, making it an authentic testimony of the actual rituals that took place at his funeral.[4] This of course does not mean that everything or every person in the scenes were exactly there at the funeral as depicted, but it clearly indicates that the intention of the scenes was to represent what had taken place at the funeral and that the scenes did not happen in the netherworld. The wailing women, in particular, would have no place in the netherworld where the deceased are already living again. The fact that the deceased was shown in the paintings as standing or sitting in various occasions did not again mean that he/she was in the netherworld, but was only a way to show that the deceased was

---

[2] Hornung (1999); Abt and Hornung (2003: 11–14). After the New Kingdom, the Amduat was no longer a royal privilege.
[3] Duell (1938, pls. 83, 87).
[4] Duell (1938, pl. 88).

**Figure 3.1** Tomb of Mereruka. Mereruka attended by mortuary priests behind him. The names of the priests are written in front of each person.
*Source*: Drawing by T. H. Huang. After Duell (1938, pl. 83).

the center of the funerary rituals and that his/her image was representing his/her spirit or soul to participate at the funeral.

Second, there were the daily life-related scenes, including domestic activities in the kitchen or in the garden, the workshops, farming and hunting scenes, harvesting, as well as public scenes such as sailing ships, with or without the participation of the deceased. The captions of these scenes reveal that certain actions were meant to please the deceased every day, like the musical scenes in the tomb of Akhethotep Hemi/Nebkauhor at Saqqara. The caption before a flautist reads "playing the flute for your [i.e. the deceased] *ka* every day."[5] This reference to the *ka* of the deceased seems to indicate that the act of playing the harp was done in the netherworld since the *ka* generally refers to the soul of the deceased. Yet many scenes only depict moments of the daily activities, and

---

[5] Strudwick (2005: 401–2).

the captions are in general a short reference to the activities, with no hint to the place where the activities took place. Presumably, it was obvious to the Egyptians that no mention is needed.

We thus face a question of whether we can interpret some paintings in the tomb as referring to the netherworld, while seeing some others as referring to life on earth or even referring to both. Could it be that this ambiguity was never felt by the Egyptians or that they felt but never resolved? Surely when they placed all the funerary objects in the tomb, there had to be an assumption that the deceased would use these objects in the netherworld. Taken as a whole, the entire tomb with its decorations and furnishings should be the place wherein the deceased would spend a life of eternity there. As we shall see in the following chapter, this idea is also implied by the common plea for people who shall pass by the tomb to make offerings and the reference in the biographic inscriptions to the stipulation of the funerary estate to ensure the continuous maintenance of the funerary cult to the deceased.

Beginning from the Middle Kingdom, in the tombs of some of the high officials, certain significant historical events were "recorded" in the wall paintings. In the tomb of Khnumhotep of the Twelfth Dynasty, for example, a group of Semites were represented. The caption reads as "37 Asiatics coming," which must be a recording of this event that was considered important in the life of Khnumhotep.[6] A group of wrestling scenes, also in the tomb of Khnumhotep, again depict a special event, perhaps something that Khnumhotep himself was fond of, so that the artist or the person who was responsible for the execution of the decoration had received the instruction to paint them to please the visitors of the tomb, perhaps also the deceased. These special scenes with possible historical significance, moreover, rule out the explanation that these are supposed to happen in the netherworld. Similarly, in the New Kingdom tombs of Senmut and Menkheperrasonb, tribute-bringing Minoans, Cretans, and Syrians were depicted, which must also have been representing actual historical situation.[7]

Without going through all the relevant paintings in the numerous tombs, it should be clear that these scenes were modeled on either the daily reality of life or a certain moment in history; thus, they could only be interpreted as intended to depict the past life of the tomb owner, although this is not to say that all the scenes were necessarily "factual representations" of the past experience of the deceased. A comparable situation in the Chinese case is the tomb decoration in

---

[6] Davies (1936, vol. I, pls. X, XI).
[7] Davies (1936, vol. I, pls. XIV, XXII, XXIII, XXIII).

the Eastern Han tomb at Holinger, Inner Mongolia, where the paintings depicted various official activities of the tomb owner, and the captions accompanying the scenes clearly indicate that "this scene depicts the Lord when he was on certain official duties."[8]

Considering the practical function of the tombs as a place where the relatives or descendants of the deceased were supposed to visit in order to make offerings and prayers, the paintings in the tombs were as much for the deceased as for the living, especially the relatives and friends, to admire the beauty of the decoration and the wealth of the family that could afford the tomb and the decoration. To this end, it is irrelevant whether the scenes, especially those showing the prosperous household and abundant harvest, were "true" or not, since they were obviously symbolic or well-wishing auspicious scenes, so to speak.

If we take into consideration the biographic texts found in the tombs since the Old Kingdom, it is also clear that the biographic texts recounted the deeds of the deceased while the deceased were alive; thus, the texts were clearly inscribed with the intention to commemorate the deceased, to demonstrate the worth and integrity of the deceased, and to serve as a testimony that qualifies the deceased to be accepted into the netherworld. This function of these texts can be seen as playing a similar role like the paintings in the tomb, that is, they all geared toward presenting a life on earth that was worthy and dignified and to allow the deceased to enjoy a good life in the netherworld.

There did not seem to be any prescribed rules for the degree of elaborations for the tomb decorations according to the ranking of the deceased. There was, as far as we can tell, no limit as to how much or how luxuriously one could or should decorate the tomb without usurping one's social or political status. One thing is for sure, that is, a private person could not build a pyramid for oneself in the Old Kingdom and Middle Kingdom for that was a royal privilege. In the New Kingdom, as both the kings and the nobles were buried in the rock-cut tombs, the differentiation was made by the extensiveness of the royal tombs (Tutankhamun's tomb excepted, as it was a salvation tomb and not the original tomb) and the decoration with various books of the netherworld.

If we accept that the paintings were depictions of the real life that the deceased could have experienced, we can also postulate that these scenes should have represented what the Egyptians considered most precious to their memories of life on earth. In other words, the scenes could be seen as representing an ideal

---

[8] Nei Menggu zizhiqu boweguan wenwu gongzuodui (1978, pl. 32).

life that the Egyptians—no doubt the well-to-do Egyptians who could afford a tomb—might have had experienced, and by all means were expecting to have in the next life.

Thus despite all these arguments for seeing the tomb paintings as basically representing the life of the living world, there is still room for the view that these scenes, particularly those "generic" scenes of daily life that were repeated in numerous variations for thousands of years, might represent the future lives in the netherworld. Indeed the graphic representation of the *Book of the Dead* Spell 110, of the Field of Offerings (Figure 3.2) that the deceased were expected to live in, shows the deceased performing exactly what a typical Egyptian farmer would do in real life: tilling the field, sowing the seeds, and harvesting the grain—all symbolic of a peaceful and bountiful life. When this scene was depicted in a New Kingdom tomb, it replaces seamlessly the traditional farming and harvesting scenes in the Old Kingdom and Middle Kingdom tombs, with the exception, of course, of the presence of the netherworld deities seen in the first register in the scene. Therefore if one wishes to argue that the scenes of daily life that we encountered numerous times in the Old Kingdom and Middle Kingdom

**Figure 3.2** Representation of the Field of Offering in the tomb of Sennedjem, copying *Book of the Dead* Spell 110.
*Source*: Open source from Metropolitan Museum (DT11771).

tombs could also represent life in the netherworld, there is really no direct counterevidence to deny it.

It is also worth noticing that the kind of ideal life depicted in the *Book of the Dead* Spell 110 has its earlier version in the Middle Kingdom *Coffin Texts* Spell 466; thus, the scribes and artisans who decorated the tomb walls could already have had certain knowledge of it, yet they chose not to represent it on the walls but left it strictly as part of the decoration of the coffins.

Moreover, since the Egyptian desert where most of the tombs were located was an arid place, a visit to the tomb will allow the spectators some enjoyment of sightseeing similar to what comic books or motion pictures brought to modern people. Life in a great mansion, in a lush farm, and on the cool Nile, as represented by the tomb paintings, could have offered the visitors some fresh sensory relief and perhaps certain secret hope that the netherworld would also be like what was depicted. The tomb paintings, in other words, were windows to an ideal world beyond the tomb, in the land of the blessed.

Lastly, the funerary objects that were supposedly for the use of the dead in the next life should also be considered together with the tomb paintings as part of the ensemble. In general, the objects consisted of real objects such as jewelry, chairs, cabinets, toiletry, clothes, and so on as well as surrogate/model objects. The models often reproduced what were depicted in the wall paintings, especially scenes of daily life, including the servants, the workshops, the houses, the tools, the ships, and so on, which constituted a set representation that complements or even duplicates the paintings (Figure 3.3). Thus if one argues that the funerary objects and models were meant to accompany the deceased to the netherworld so as to create a comfortable life, the paintings on the wall would also carry similar functions, as Hayes said, "in the belief that these presentments of reality were endowed with the essence of the originals and would supply him with his needs for all time." The appearance of the offering lists in the tombs, furthermore, indicates that the objects in the list were intended to be offered to the deceased as sustenance in the netherworld.[9] Whether the list really recorded the funerary objects supplied in the tomb is a moot question. Archaeologists rarely have any chance to identify the objects listed with actual findings in the tombs for obvious reasons: the looting of the tombs made it impossible. As a comparative note, in the Han Dynasty Mawangdui tomb no. 1, which shall be discussed later, there was a list of funerary objects called Qiance (遣策). Since this tomb was not looted before, archaeologists were curious about whether the objects

---

[9] Barta (1962); Morales (2015).

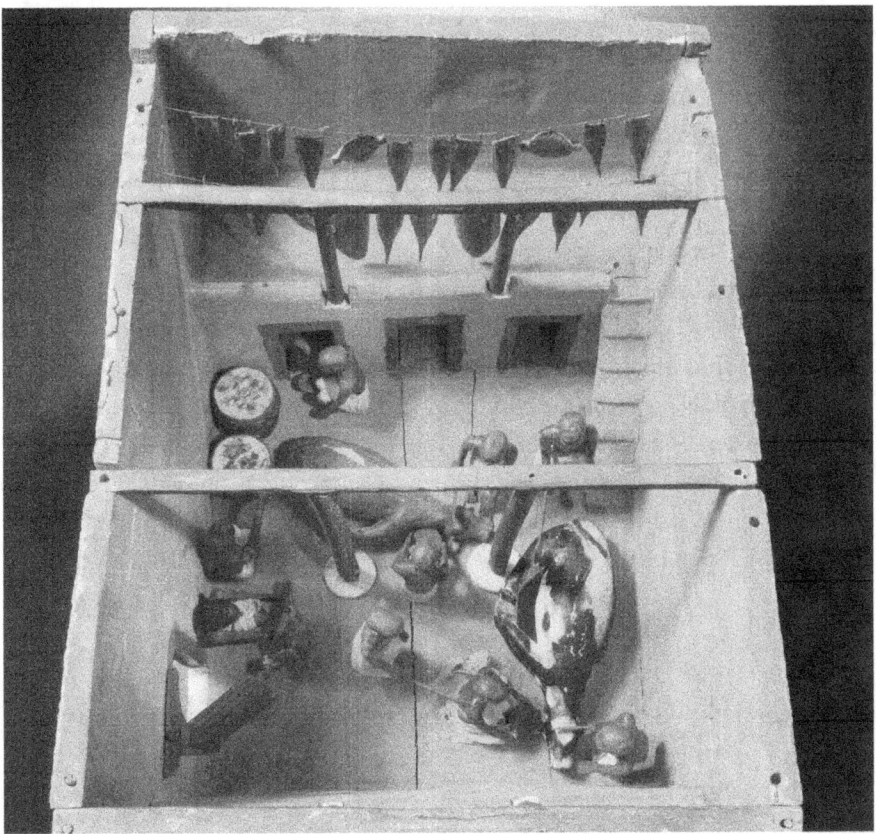

**Figure 3.3** Model of a slaughterhouse that echoes the tomb paintings depicting kitchen scenes.
*Source*: Open source from Metropolitan Museum (DP 351556).

listed on the Qiance matched those excavated from the tomb. The answer was negative. Whatever the reasons might have been, at least this reference places our evaluation of the Egyptian offering list in a better perspective.

Moreover, models of people and houses, boats, and workshops were never listed in the offering lists. The appeal of the deceased to the living who shall pass by the tomb to make a verbal offering of "a thousand of incense, a thousand of alabaster and clothing, oxen and fowl, oryxes and antelopes" echoes the offering list as a generic formula that did not correspond to reality.

Our final assessment of the tomb style, tomb painting, and funerary objects, therefore, must rest on the assumption that, allowing the reasonable understanding of the paintings as representing life on earth, the entire ensemble of the funerary setup was meant for the deceased to enjoy a good life in the netherworld. By depicting various scenes of daily life, such as hunting, fishing, harvesting, and handcraft production in the household, the Egyptians were engaging in a visual representation of a world that they were familiar with, that is, as far as the decorations on the tomb chamber walls of the nobles and officials are concerned, all the scenes could be seen as modeling on the real-life events. Note especially that, with a few exceptions such as the tomb of Senndjem, no divine beings appear to have been present in any of the scenes in the private tombs. We emphasize this point because beginning from the New Kingdom, the royal tombs were decorated with scenes of religious nature devoid of any daily life scenes,[10] thus emphasizing the otherworldly nature of the decoration.

The kind of life in the netherworld, moreover, would be similar to the life of a prosperous person on earth, except, as the *Coffin Texts* and the *Book of the Dead* had described, the deceased would have to overcome a number of obstacles during his/her journey to the final destination, the Field of Offerings, as described in Spell 110 of the *Book of the Dead*. This assessment will be examined further when we discuss textual evidence and compare with the Chinese material.

## The Netherworld in Han Chinese Graphic Representations

### The Mawangdui Paintings

It has been pointed out in Chapter 2 that the evolution of tomb style in early China from the vertical pit wooden casket tomb to the horizontal brick tomb and the changing combination of funerary assemblage from ritual bronze vessels to surrogate models of objects for daily use suggest a trend toward a more realistic imagination of the netherworld based on this world. This imitation was shown first by the construction of a home-like tomb for the deceased to live in and then by providing the deceased with the necessities of daily life in the form of surrogate models.[11] Moreover, the change in burial styles and funerary assemblage corresponded to, firstly, the disintegration of the Shang-Zhou political and ritual structure and the decline of the old nobilities associated with the vassal system and blood relations and, secondly, the rise of a new social class in association with the development of bureaucracy and meritocracy.[12] As we can see from the previous discussions, the development in tomb style and

---

[10] Hornung (1999); Darnell (2018).
[11] Poo (2011a); Pirazzoli-T'Serstevens (2009).
[12] Poo (1993, chapter 2); Huang (2003); Lai (2015).

the use of funerary objects of daily life were paralleled by the Egyptian case. Thus one could assume that the netherworld in the imagination of the Han people was more or less the same as this world. While this may not be far off the truth, it could only be part of the truth. One well-known example that shows the rich imagination of a world beyond this life is the funerary silk paintings/banners found in the Mawangdui tombs no. 1 and no. 3, dated to late second century BCE.[13]

The archaeological site of Mawangdui, present-day Changsha, Hunan Province, was made famous by the discovery of three tombs of the Marquis Dai family (Figure 3.4). Tomb no. 1 belonged to Lady Xin Zhui, wife of Marquis Dai, tomb no. 2 belonged to the Marquis himself and dated to 186 BCE, and tomb no. 3 most likely belonged to her son and dated to 168 BCE. Both tomb no. 1 and tomb no. 3 produced abundant objects as well as a number of silk paintings that constituted one of the most important archaeological discoveries in twentieth-century China. The well-preserved body of Lady Dai, moreover, was no less than a wonder to our knowledge of the ancient Chinese way of burial.

The Egyptian mastaba or the rock-cut tombs had the natural advantage of having hard surface that could be painted or carved with reliefs so that they could be preserved for thousands of years. The Chinese vertical pit wooden casket tombs, on the other hand, did not have the quality to last long; thus, whatever decorations that might have donned the wooden caskets were doomed to perish after a certain period of time. It was extremely rare if any decoration in a vertical pit tomb could be preserved. The silk paintings found in tomb no. 1 and tomb no. 3 at Mawangdui were therefore exceptions among exceptions. We do not know how popular or prevalent such kind of paintings were used by the people of Han to decorate their tombs, but it can be certain that the Mawangdui paintings were not unique in the Han funerary culture, and parallels could be found in other parts of China and in different time periods, as we shall discuss later. In fact the term "decoration" might be somewhat misleading, as at least in the cases of the T-shaped silk paintings found in Mawangdui tomb no. 1 and tomb no. 3, the painting was most likely some kind of ritual banner to identify the deceased, and it was placed on the top of the coffin when it was entombed, indicating a close relationship with the deceased in the coffin. The function of the paintings, therefore, was mainly religious rather than simply decorative. The

---

[13] Hunansheng bowuguan and Zhongguo kexueyuan kaogu yanjiusuo (1973), Hunansheng bowuguan and Hunan sheng wenwu gaogu yanjiusuo (2004). For a detailed study of the painting in tomb no. 1, see Loewe (1979).

**Figure 3.4** The T-shaped painting on silk from Mawangdui tomb no. 1. Courtesy of Hunan Provincial Museum.
*Source*: Hunan sheng bowuguan and Zhongguo kexueyuan kaogu yanjiusuo, eds., *Changsha mawangdui ihao hanmu* (Beijing: Wenwu chubanshe, 1973, vol. 1, fig. 38).

identity of the T-shaped painting or banner has been a continuous subject of debate among scholars, and the most convincing explanation is that it was, or served as the substitute of, the "name banner" that identifies the deceased in the funeral setting. Thus although textual evidence of the "name banner" refers to a piece of cloth with the actual name of the deceased written on it, the Mawangdui painting seems to be a local variation of such a name banner, perhaps an "image banner" that functions the same as a name banner.[14]

The T-shaped silk painting found in tomb no. 1 (Figure 3.4) is about 205 cm long, with a width of 92 cm for the upper part and 47.7 cm for the lower part. The shape actually resembles that of a dress, though it is only a single piece of cloth. In the middle of the painting stood an old lady who, with a staff in her hand and receiving offerings from two servant-like persons, has generally been identified as the tomb owner Lady Dai herself.[15]

Although some of the elements found in the painting, such as the toad and hare in the moon, the sunbird, the *fusang* tree, and the eight red dots among the tree leaves, could be identified with known textual traditions in connection with the legend of the Queen Mother of the West and the myth about Hou Yi, the hero who shot down nine suns in the sky, a number of elements still defy interpretation. These include the Herculean "giant" who holds the lower platform, the person at the top of the painting with a coiling snake tail, the two "officials" waiting at the "gate" to "heaven," and the strange bird above the head of Lady Dai.[16] On the whole, it is relatively certain that, with the image of the deceased tomb owner in the center, the silk painting depicts the world where the deceased would be going to or residing in. Yet this world does not look like any ordinary daily life setting, such as those daily life scenes often found in the Egyptian tombs.

Moreover, the decorations on the four layers of coffins of Lady Dai also deserve analyses, since each of them has a design that suggests certain visualization of the netherworld. The outer coffin was painted black, the color of night and death. As a passage in an Eastern Han tomb inscription remarked, the dead entered "a long night that could not see the sun and the stars, their spirits all alone, turning to the darkness below and separated from their family."[17] Thus symbolically the dead are encased in this darkness that separates the living and the dead. The second coffin is painted with intricate designs of clouds and a large number of

---

[14] For a full argument, see Wu (1992).
[15] For detailed discussions, see Loewe (1979: 30–59); Wu (1992); Wang (2011).
[16] For a very compelling study, see Wang (2011).
[17] Nanyangshi bowuguan (1974).

curious spirits or demonic figures that emerge out of the clouds. The fluid and graceful lines of the clouds and the bodily movement of the figures produce a peaceful, vivid, yet dream-like realm that suggests a nonhuman world high up in the sky inhabited by these figures.

The third coffin, with a red background, has pictures of clouds, dragons, tigers, phoenixes, deer, and winged immortals. The main theme of the design on the third coffin, different from the cloud design on the second coffin, seems to suggest an environment where some of the most auspicious animals are inhabited, indicating a realm of blissfulness and happiness and thus a region that the deceased may aspire to join.

The innermost coffin returns to simplicity, with geometric designs on the cover, red paint inside, and black paint outside, as if to show that the dead now live in a bright daylight within the darkness of night, that is, Lady Dai would have her own "life" in the enveloping darkness of death. The four layers of coffins, therefore, could be seen as metaphorical representations of the several regions that the deceased would go through during the journey to his/her destination: first comes pitch black, as death occurs; then gradually there appear clouds, in which spirits, monsters, and animals of all sorts reside; passing through this cloudy region the deceased enters into a realm of blissfulness and happiness; and finally reaches his/her home of eternal sunshine. Having said so, however, it should be clear that, whether or not the above observation could elucidate the significance of the designs on the coffins, we cannot afford not to make some sense out of such rich imageries.[18]

It is remarkable that the coffins are assembled in a very precise way, using dovetails instead of nails to connect the boards that were able to resist air for two thousand years. This must have contributed to the remarkably well-preserved body of Lady Dai. According to chemical analysis, the reason why her body was able to resist decay was because the limited oxygen in the coffin was quickly consumed during the initial decaying process. When this happens, the interior of the coffin becomes oxygen free and thus no microbiotic activity could have happened. Obviously, with such elaborate craftsmanship, these coffins were unlikely to be commissioned by the deceased's family only after her death. They were most probably made while the would-be occupant was still alive, as was the custom of the rich during this period. The Eastern Han scholar Wang Fu once uttered a protest against the contemporary funerary custom: "To make a set of coffins requires thousands of craftsmen, and when they were finished they might

---

[18] Cf. Wu Hung (1992: 133–4); Wu Hung (2010: 127–31); Tseng (2011: 166–9); Wang (2011).

weigh ten thousand *jin*, which could not be lifted without many people, and could not be moved without a large cart."[19] Though written during the Eastern Han, what he described seems to be true also for the Western Han period. Many other tombs of the same style excavated by modern archaeologists before or after the Mawangdui tombs demonstrate this point clearly.

Another T-shaped painted banner similar to the one in Lady Dai's tomb was found in Mawangdui tomb no. 3. Except for the central figure, which was replaced by a male figure, presumably the deceased tomb owner and Lady Dai's son, all other details in this painting were almost found in the painting of tomb no. 1. This indicates that such paintings must have been produced by the same workshop and could very well have been part of the standard funerary paraphernalia of the time. It also shows that the images in the painting were not arbitrary creations but meaningful icons that were carefully chosen for specific purposes.

In addition to the scenes of otherworldly nature, two other silk paintings were found hanging on the eastern and western walls of the tomb no. 3 chamber: one depicting daily life and the other a display of chariots. Though these paintings are rare samples of early Chinese paintings on silk, the subjects painted can also be found in later tomb paintings as standard decorative themes.

Here we encounter similar issues as we did in reading the Egyptian tomb paintings: were they representations of any "reality" related to the tomb owner's life? As there are no captions attached to the paintings, we can only speculate upon the intention of these paintings. Given the status of the tomb owner, it is reasonable to see him in action as a military commander of some sort. The painting of chariots seems to depict a scene of military parade, as rows of chariots were greeted by several officials kneeling to the left of the painting. Whether the tomb owner himself was in the first row facing the kneeling officials is impossible to say. Whereas in the boating scene, it is equally impossible to determine if it was a representation of reality of some event that happened in the life of the tomb owner (Figure 3.5). In general, in the Han tomb decorations, biographical references are rarely found. An example is the wall painting in an Eastern Han brick tomb found at Holinger, Inner Mongolia.[20] The paintings depicted on the walls are accompanied by explanatory captions that relate to the various offices that the tomb owner, a military leader, had held throughout his life. Yet even though the captions may refer to certain reality such as offices

---

[19] Wang Fu (1971: 15).
[20] Nei Menggu zizhiqu boweguan wenwu gongzuodui (1978).

**Figure 3.5** A fragment of a boating scene on a silk cloth found in Mawangdui tomb no. 3.
*Source*: Line drawing by T. H. Huang. After Jin Weino and Nie Chongzheng (2009: 10).

held by the tomb owner, the scenes may still be following contain conventional decorative schemes.

All told, the images on the Mawangdui silk paintings and the coffins could be seen as an effort to represent an imaginary landscape of the world of the dead that integrated different ideas—whether religious, mythological, or legendary—that were circulating in early Han. What is worth noticing is that the Mawangdui silk paintings—meaning the T-shaped silk banners found in tomb no. 1 and tomb no. 3 plus the "wall paintings" placed on the wall of the wooden casket of tomb no. 3—are the products of a decorative tradition that encompassed the vertical pit wooden casket tombs and the painted brick tombs. A similar silk painting, for example, was found in a vertical pit tomb in Shandong (Figure 3.6).[21]

---

[21] Linyi Jinqueshan Hanmu fajuezu (1977); for discussion, see Li Xiaoxuan 李小旋 (2016).

**Figure 3.6** A silk painting found in an early Han tomb discovered at Jinqueshan, Linyi.
*Source*: Line drawing by T. H. Huang. After Linyi Jinqueshan Hanmu fajuezu (1977: 11, inside cover).

This painting, measuring 200 by 40 cm, of a size similar to the Mawangdui paintings, shows the sun with the black bird and the moon with the toad on the top, two coiling dragons at the bottom, and five registers of human figures in the middle. The basic structure and mythological allusions, therefore, are quite similar to those of the Mawangdui silk paintings. In the middle part with five registers under the roof, the top register shows a woman, possibly the tomb owner, as she was depicted in a larger figure compared to the four attendants facing her. The four registers below were depicting scenes of daily life: playing music, receiving guests, spinning, and so on. It can therefore be understood as a further development of the middle scene of the Mawangdui silk paintings (with the standing Lady Dai or her son) and that this painting could represent a half-way development toward the later tomb paintings that profusely depicted scenes of daily life. The idea of depicting the tomb owner and some daily activities—whether in this or next world is impossible to say—is therefore quite similar to the Egyptian tomb decorative schemes.

When we look at the decorative paintings in the late Western Han brick tomb of Bu Qianqiu in Loyang, the similarities in the choice of mythological themes demonstrate a widespread and long-lasting decorative tradition that reveals a common conception of the netherworld. For example, the ceiling was painted with the sun (with a bird) on the one end and the moon (with a toad) on the other end. There were also the figures of the mythological characters of Fuxi and Nüwa, both in human shape with serpent-like lower bodies, and other figures of gods or immortals, which are comparable to some of the figures in the silk paintings in the Mawangdui tomb no. 1 and tomb no. 3. A woman, presumably the wife of the tomb owner, was shown riding on a three-headed bird. A man, presumably Bu Qianqiu himself, thus the counterpart of Lady Dai or her son in the Mawangdui paintings, was shown riding on a flying serpent.[22] Both figures are comparable to the central figures of the Mawangdui silk paintings.

In another late Western Han brick tomb found at Xi'an, the ceiling was covered with a picture of the heavenly bodies, including the hare and the toad in the moon, the bird in the sun, and the twenty-eight constellations. On the walls are painted natural landscapes and cranes and tigers, elements that also appear in the Mawangdui silk paintings.[23] Thus it is legitimate to assume that these paintings, whether on the silk banners or on the ceilings of the brick

---

[22] Sun Zuoyun (1977).
[23] Shaanxisheng kaogu yanjiusuo and Xian Jiaotong daxue 西安交通大學 (1991: 49–51).

tombs, serve as symbolic representations of some of the elements of the world in which the deceased were expected to dwell. The similarities of the motifs and vocabularies of images among these funerary decorations suggest that they belonged to a tradition of funerary art that incorporated some commonly held ideas concerning the world of the dead.[24] The position of the Mawangdui silk painting, which covers the coffin just like the ceiling of the brick tomb, moreover, makes the silk paintings comparable to the ceiling paintings of the tomb of Bu Qianqiu and the Xian tomb, as they all allude to a heavenly sphere decorated with the sun, the moon, and the constellations.[25] It should be evident that the paintings all refer to the heavenly sphere that the deceased was supposed to travel to or through. An earlier example of silk painting shows a man riding on a dragon, presumably a gesture of ascending to heaven. This painting is also found in the same general area of the ancient Chu state where the Mawangdui tombs are located.[26] It is unclear, however, if this painting was used in a similar funerary context.

In sum, one could make a case that the Mawangdui paintings might have represented a decorative tradition that is the precursor of the painted brick tombs in later history. It should be emphasized, however, that this imagination of the netherworld was the result of a collective wisdom, distilled from the life experience of generations of people, something that should not be dismissed easily as simply "imagination" without depth of meaning. However, it is also important that we should not be overzealous to try to pin down every detail in the paintings and tie them to a perfect scheme of journey to or description of the netherworld. It is reasonable to simply regard that those elements represented in the paintings or wall reliefs as auspicious symbols, indicating a well-wish for the deceased in an uncertain future life. Uncertain, apparently, was the case about if and where there was a netherworld waiting for the deceased.[27] The coexistence of different traditions was not contradictory, but a way to ensure that the deceased will have a safe passage. The implication of this realization calls the need to investigate the changing value system that caused this change.

---

[24] See Poo (1993: 134–8). A convenient index of the decorative themes in Han tombs can be found in Finsterbusch (1966–2000). See also Huang (2008, chapter 2).
[25] See Loyangshi dier wenwu gongzuodui, Huang Minglan, and Guo Yinqiang (1996: 12).
[26] Wenwu chubanshe (1973).
[27] Poo (1990). For a comprehensive publication of Han Tomb reliefs and paintings, see Zongguo huaxiangshi quanji bianji weiyuanhui (1997); Finsterbusch (1966–2000).

## Painted Brick Tombs

The trend for the change of tomb styles in the Han Dynasty was that the curve of the use of vertical pit wooden casket tombs goes down and that the curve of the use of horizontal brick tombs goes up, with the middle Western Han as a crossing point.[28] With the increasing use of horizontal brick tombs, a tradition of tomb decoration began to emerge. The use of stones or bricks in building the tomb, just like the Mastaba, made it easier for the artisans to plan and decorate the walls with pictures, painted bricks, molded bricks, or stone reliefs.

The subjects depicted in the tomb decorations in the early western Han period represented by the silk paintings in the Mawangdui tombs were mostly mythological subjects and seemed to indicate that the deceased were ascending to a heavenly abode, accompanied by mythical creatures and deities, as well as symbols of immortality, represented by the Chang-O myth. In early Chinese mythology, the story of Chang-O was related to the Queen Mother of the West, the possessor of the elixir of immortality, which Chang-O stole and ascended to the moon.[29]

Yet there was little indication of the Queen Mother's role as a deity in the netherworld, although tomb decorations often show traces of her image and those associated with her, such as the hare, the moon, and the toad in the moon; the nine-tailed fox; and so on.[30] The cult of the Queen Mother of the West was basically a cult of immortality, which was an aspiration against death and therefore should have nothing to do with the world after death.[31] Presumably the inclusion of these images in tomb decorations was symbolic of a blessed afterlife, even though it should have happened in the realm of the Queen Mother in the Western region.

The winged immortals on the painted coffins of Lady Dai also suggested a similar idea that the deceased were living among the immortals. This kind of scene of a realm of immortality or a heavenly abode was the dominating theme of the tomb decoration of Western Han. They appear in both the vertical pit tombs and the early brick tombs, indicating that the changing of tomb style did not immediately affect the tradition of decoration. Beginning from late Western Han, scenes of daily life appeared in the painted brick tombs and by the Eastern Han they were the dominant subjects in tomb decoration.[32] However, it must be

---

[28] Poo (1993: 12, figs. 1–6).
[29] Yu Yingshi (1964); Poo (1998a, chapter 7).
[30] See Liu Zhiyuan (1958, fig. 67).
[31] Fracasso (1988).
[32] Huang (2008, chapter 2).

emphasized that the elements of mythological symbols and immortality did not disappear completely but often blended in with the scenes of daily life.

How then should one interpret the scenes? Are they depictions of the world after death? It seems clear that the mythological scenes suggest that the deceased shall go to a heavenly realm, with little resemblance of the world of the living. However, the funerary objects discovered in the tombs suggest a different world. This world was more in line with the intention or function of the funerary objects; that is, this world after death was more or less like the world of the living. The funerary objects were intended for the deceased to use, and the scenes of daily life depict the occasion where the objects were put to use: utensils for the banquets, musical instruments for the scenes of dancing and music performance, and figurines of servants for attending the need of the deceased in all occasions. The question is similar to what we ask of the Egyptian tomb paintings, whether the daily life scenes were reflections and reminiscence of the past life of the tomb owner on earth or anticipation of the new life that he/she might lead in the netherworld.

When, occasionally, captions on the tomb painting are preserved, there is a greater chance for us to determine the intention of the decoration. In the Eastern Han tomb found at Holiger, for example, the paintings depicted on the walls are accompanied by explanatory captions that relate to the various offices that the tomb owner, a military leader, had held throughout his life.[33] Thus we are sure that the scenes were meant to be biographic, much like the scenes depicting the coming of the Semites and Minoans in the Egyptian tombs. Yet even though the captions may refer to certain real-life situations such as offices held, the representations may still be following contain conventional way of decorative schemes. With examples like the Holinger tomb, it should be clear that the paintings and decorations found in the tombs could serve different purposes depending upon the status of the tomb owner and the size of the tomb. Even in the same tomb there still could be scenes of daily life mixed with scenes of otherworldly or mythological nature. In the Holinger tomb, examples of mythical creatures such as the white wolf, the divine mushroom, the jade sheep, the crane, the white elephant, and so on were depicted, which might have served as auspicious symbols.

In order to interpret the tomb decorations such as the references to the heavenly abode or the world of the immortals, we need to take a look at the intellectual and religious background that nurtured the development of the

---

[33] Nei Menggu zizhiqu wenwu kaugu yanjiuso (2007).

funerary culture of China. The traditional understanding of China during the Han was that it was a period when the Confucian humanistic values became the central and dominating ideology of the state.[34] While this might be true to a certain extent, as the learning and teaching of the Confucian classics became the most important avenue for a person to succeed in society and to ascend to the officialdom—similar to what the Egyptian elder Ptahhotep had hoped for his son, there were also parallel and competing ideologies such as Daoism and the Legalist tradition that had developed since the Warring States period. The Confucian teaching, while concentrating on the issues of human values and the morality and ethics for building a harmonious society, did not pay too much attention to the need of the general public to know more about the world after death, the world in heaven, or the mythological world that had been passed down over the generations. Confucius was famously quoted as saying: "Without knowing life, how could we know about death?" As well as death, Confucius also did not like to discuss subjects related to "the strange, the violent, the chaotic, and the spiritual." The fact that these "non-Confucian" subjects were mentioned but dismissed, yet not denied, indicates implicitly that these were what interested people in his time and perhaps in all times. This leaves room for speculation on the fate of a person after death and speculations that could have combined any number of religious or mythological understandings about what this world after death would look like. The subjects depicted on the silk banner found in the Mawangdui tombs and other places, therefore, were not new to their time, but most probably based on traditions passed down from long ago. We shall return to this in the next chapter when we examine textual sources regarding the idea of the netherworld.

## Comparative Note

Broadly speaking, the paintings and decorations in the Chinese tombs present two different worlds: the world of the living, including many categories but certainly not every imaginable activity in people's daily life, and the world of the immortals, deities, and mythical creatures. Yet questions arise with such division, since the two worlds often intersected or mixed in the representations, so that a clear separation between the two can be difficult. It might be possible to solve this difficulty by admitting that the scenes in the tombs all represent

---

[34] Nylan (2001).

some aspects of the netherworld, in which there are features resembling this world—for example, all the daily activities—and features that belonged not to this world but another mythical place where those otherworldly creatures and deities resides. But we also need to take into account of the possibility that some of the scenes were biographical, reflecting the life history of the deceased. At least these could not be interpreted as representing the netherworld.

It is also useful to note that many of the scenes, whether those of the daily life type or the mythical type, were often made into individual molded bricks and used as decorations and as auspicious signs that could bring good luck to the deceased. In fact the use of molded bricks as decorations in the tombs suggests that for the people who constructed the tombs, the function of the scenes was mostly decorative, with the additional function as auspicious signs intended to bring good luck for the deceased. Given this understanding, it is perfectly reasonable that scenes of daily life could be mixed with scenes of otherworldly nature, since they all meant to be beneficial for the deceased. Whether they meant to depict the netherworld where the dead were supposed to go, however, was probably a question that was not asked and did not have a definite answer.

For the Egyptian tomb paintings, similarly, the daily scenes could become more or less stereotypical presentations, sometimes as part of the larger scheme of decoration regarding the distribution of different types of scenes in different rooms.[35] The craftsmen who worked on the decorations would most probably have a master plan in hand for reference, to arrange the scenes according to the space available. However, as discussed earlier, the captions could be either general descriptions of the activities or specific references to the names of people attending the funeral or events that the deceased had experienced when alive. Thus it is also inconclusive whether we should regard the scenes as representing the netherworld or this world. Both possibilities could be true given that the tomb was, after all, the place where the deceased were supposed to live, and that this place was basically modeled on the world of the living.

When compared with the Chinese tomb paintings, it can be said that the mood of the scenes in both the Egyptian and the Chinese tomb paintings is in general positive, representing the cheerful, prosperous side of the daily life, thus with the intention of presenting an optimistic prospect for the deceased. As suggested earlier, the paintings or decorations were windows to the world beyond the tomb, where the deceased was expected to reside. With this intention, it is

---

[35] For a detailed study comparing the decorative schemes of Han tombs and Egyptian Old Kingdom tombs, see Huang (2015).

also understandable that the difficulties or dangers that the deceased might be encountering in this future life would not become the subject of presentation. This of course does not mean that people did not have certain apprehensions regarding the netherworld. For this, the textual sources provide us with more concrete evidence, as we shall discuss in the next chapter.

# 4

# Textual Representations of the Netherworld

In addition to the graphic representations, various funerary texts also provide rich material for our understanding of the Egyptian imagination of the netherworld. On the whole, the netherworld was described as a sequence of regions that the dead were supposed to pass through, and in each region, there were different obstacles consisting of a number of enemies and demons, intermixed with helpers and deities who made sure that the deceased would pass through difficulties and reach their destination. This destination was variously known as the Beautiful West, the Field of Offerings, or the Rosetau, the realm of Osiris, ruler of the netherworld. These will be analyzed in the following against the social and natural environments of ancient Egypt.

As for the Chinese materials, in addition to tomb decorations, texts found in tombs often reveal people's concerns with the life of the deceased in the netherworld. For example, some texts referred to the world of the dead as managed by a host of bureaucrats, and taxes and household registrations were required in this underworld bureaucratic society. Thus the details of the netherworld in China seem to be more or less conditioned by this-worldly experience. A comparison between both visions and their relationship with the life experience would enable us to gain further insight into the nature of each culture.

## Textual Representations of the Egyptian Netherworld

To complement the material testimony of a tremendous effort to construct a visible world of the dead, we shall turn to written texts. The funerary texts of the Old Kingdom period provide us with descriptions of an imaginary world of the dead that is worth analyzing. The tomb inscriptions usually consist of biographical information of the tomb owner, as well as other information that the tomb owner or the descendants who built the tomb deemed useful or meaningful to be included in the tomb, such as certain legal documents[1] or even a letter from the king.[2] Among these tomb inscriptions are some expressions that, though sound stereotypical, could actually be regarded as representing a collective imagination concerning the netherworld.

One type of formulaic expressions in the tombs of the Old Kingdom period is the so-called appeals to the living, as it often begins with invocations such as "O you who live on earth, … who shall pass by this tomb of mine of the necropolis, may you give bread, beer, and water."[3] These invocations were usually addressed to those who shall pass by the tomb, urging them to make some offerings to the deceased. In return, the deceased would offer protection to those who did some favor to the dead. On the other hand, if the passerby somehow entered the tomb with impurity, whether in thought or in actual physical state, or even damaged the tomb, the tomb owner also promised retaliation:

> With regard to any man who shall do anything evil to my tomb, or who shall enter it with the intention of stealing, I shall seize his neck like a bird's, and I shall be judged with him in the court of the Great God.[4]

The prevalence of such formulaic expressions makes it certain that the assumption of a life hereafter, the assumption that there could be a connection between the living and the dead and that the deed of the living could be subjected to a certain kind of judgment administered by the gods, was a common perception in society.

In this regard, that is, the protection of the tomb, it is notable that legal texts were sometimes included in the tomb. Examples such as the decrees for setting up the estates in the tomb of Metjen (Fourth Dynasty) or the text in the tomb of Kaiemnefret (Fifth Dynasty) that stipulates the duty of the mortuary priests for the deceased's funerary cult and the penalty for those priests who did not carry out their proper duty[5] indicate what the deceased were concerned about. In the New Kingdom, the famous text "Duties of the Vizier" found in the tomb of Rehkmire,[6] although not strictly a legal text but a decree of King Thutmosis III, carries the authority of law. By posting this text, the tomb owner

---

[1] Such as the tomb inscription of Metjen relating to the setting up of his estate. *Urk* I: 1–7; Goedicke (1970: 5–20); Strudwick (2005: 192–4).
[2] Such as the biographical inscription of Harkhuf that contains the letter of Pepi II; *Urk* I: 121–30; Strudwick (2005: 328–33).
[3] Garnot (1938).
[4] Strudwick (2005: 220).
[5] Strudwick (2005, paragraph nos. 106, 108).
[6] Lichtheim (1976: 21–4).

Rehkmire demonstrated his personal prestige that certainly carried some weight in protecting the tomb.

We can regard these legal texts as part of the tomb decoration that was designed to impress those who came into the tomb with the prestige and status of the deceased and to urge them to behave benevolently toward the tomb and its owner. Occasionally even when the deceased testified that he had paid the workmen in full for the work that they performed to build the tomb, a bit of warning was also added to the potentially malicious people who might do harm to the tomb: "My lord did this for me especially so that I might be *imahku*. (With regard to) him who shall do anything evil to it (the tomb), I shall be judged with him on this matter by the Great God. I satisfied the craftsman in respect of that which he did."[7] In a sense, the legal language could have served as some kind of protection to the tomb itself.

This connection or perceived interaction between the living and the dead is further demonstrated by a genre of text known as the "letter to the dead" that began to appear in the Old Kingdom period.[8] Such letters were usually written by the living to deceased relatives, whether a spouse, a sibling, or a parent. The content of such letters was usually very specific, as the living had certain complaints, such as property disputes among the kinsfolk or unjust treatment by others, to address the deceased and ask for help. The most interesting aspect of such letters, besides revealing to us the realistic picture of the daily life of the people, is that the living addressed the deceased as if both parties were alive as before. Undeniably, there was a common belief among the living that this complaint letter could reach the deceased and that the deceased somehow possessed certain power to help the living. These were not prayers to invoke blessings from the ancestors, but blunt demands for help based on past exchanges of favors. For example, a son complained to his deceased mother that he was harmed by another dead person, apparently with the intention to implore the mother to do something, since he had been a good son:

> Shepsi addresses his mother Iyu: This [letter] is a reminder of this which you said to me, your son: "Bring me quails that I may eat them"; and I, your son brought you seven quails and you ate them [all]. Am I being injured right in your presence so that my children are discontent with me, your son who is [himself] ill? Who will pour water for you? If only you would decide between me and Sebekhotep, whom I brought from another town to be buried in his

---

[7] Strudwick (2005, paragraph no. 184).
[8] Basic reference is Gardiner and Sethe (1928).

town among his tomb-companions, having given him funerary clothing. Why does he act against me, your son? I have neither said nor done anything wrong to him. Wrongdoing is painful to the gods![9]

Several interesting points could be found in this letter. First, there was an assumption that a deceased mother could hold some kind of judgment in the netherworld to help her son. Was this because of her status in the family even when she was alive or because she was an "honored spirit" since she was dead? The kind of petty quarrels that the son was seeking justice for, moreover, indicates a very intimate imagination of life in the netherworld. The daily chores and complains that common people experienced were carried over into the netherworld with no apparent difference. The assumption also implies that the social environment in the netherworld was imagined based on the model of the living. However, as we shall see in the following, life in the netherworld as depicted in the funerary text did not seem to be as "daily life"-like as the situation depicted in the letter to the dead.

Based on the material discussed earlier as well as the conceptual construction of the netherworld, it is possible now to look at the burials holistically. On the one hand, the structure of the mastaba and later also the rock-cut tombs, with the common feature of chambers in small or large numbers, inevitably resembled or symbolized a kind of living quarters for the dead. As the Egyptians themselves referred to them appropriately, they were the "house of eternity (*pr n nḥḥ*)." The various wall paintings that depicted the daily life of the deceased in his/her mansion or estate, whether imaginary or not, help to build up this concrete picture of the world that the dead were going to be residing in. Thus there were visual and physical factors involved in the construction of the netherworld, which were imagined and manifested in the physical existence of the tomb.

On the other hand, this construction of the netherworld went beyond the mere material and concrete existence of a physical space. It was also conceived as a world where there was a system of meanings in operation and where there were rules or morals to be followed. Thus it resembled the world of the living, as this world also constituted a web of meanings. The funerary texts, including the "appeals to the living," "the letter to the dead," or threats to unfriendly intruders, collectively suggested that in the imagination of the Egyptians, the netherworld was a place operating on certain principles similar to the world of

---

[9] Strudwick (2005: 183).

the living. Moreover, there was a ubiquitous formula that usually appeared on the doorframe of the tomb:

> An offering which the king gives and an offering which Anubis, who is on his mountain, who dwells in the divine tent-shrine, who is in his wrappings, the lord of the sacred land gives that he might be buried in the necropolis of the western desert, having grown old most perfectly as an *imakhu* in the sight of the Great God.[10]

This formula established the legal and social position of the dead in both worlds: the king made a gift to the deceased in recognition of his service in life and the god of the cemetery Anubis made a gift to ensure that the deceased could have his/her necessary sustenance in the western land of the dead. Thus the tomb was both the converging point of the world of the living and the dead and also a departing point that separated the two worlds.

## The *Pyramid Texts*

It remains to be discussed about the most extensive and complicated funerary texts that the Old Kingdom had produced—the *Pyramid Texts*.[11] These royal funerary texts, for they appeared only in the royal pyramids after the Fifth Dynasty, had been the center of attention of scholars who study Egyptian religion, as they contain a vast amount of information on the Egyptian religious beliefs and cosmologies. It is not easy to summarize the content of these texts, suffice it to say that they contain ritual texts pronounced during the royal funeral, later inscribed on the walls of the burial chamber and other subsidiary chambers and corridors of the pyramids. These texts could be roughly divided into two broad categories: one, to revive the deceased to become a living spirit so as to join his/her ancestors/gods in the netherworld; two, to protect the deceased against any threat or malicious attack during his/her journey toward that destination.

After the offering ritual and mouth-opening ritual had been performed for the king, a resurrection ritual followed. Allusions to the place where the king shall travel to after resurrection could be found in the ritual text:

> Ho, Unis! You have not gone away dead: you have gone away alive. Sit on Osiris's chair, with your baton in your arm, and govern the living; With your water-lily

---

[10] Strudwick (2005: 328).
[11] For an introduction, see Allen (2005: 1–14).

scepter in your arm, and govern those of the inaccessible places. Your lower arms are of Atum, your upper arms of Atum, your belly of Atum, your back of Atum, your rear of Atum, your legs of Atum, your face of Anubis. Horus's mounds shall serve you; Seth's mounds shall serve you.

Ho, Unis! Beware of the lake! RECITATION 4 TIMES.

Dispatches of your *ka* have come for you, dispatches of your father have come for you, dispatches of the Sun have come for you, (saying): "Go in the wake of your Sun and become clean, your bones falcon-goddesses in the sky, that you may exist beside the god, and leave your house to your son of your begetting."

But you shall become clean in the cool waters of the stars and board (the sunboat) on cords of metal, on the shoulders of Horus in his identity of the one who is in Sokar's boat.

The populace will cry out to you once the Imperishable Stars have raised you aloft.

Climb to the place where your father is, where Geb is, and he will give you what is on Horus's brow. You shall become *akh* through it, you shall take control through it, you shall be through it at the fore of the westerners.[12]

The gist of the ritual texts quoted previously is to announce that the king was not dead but instead was revived and became Osiris, and at the same time was also identified with the primordial god Atum. The place where he shall reside after resurrection was in heaven, and he shall ride in the boat of the sun god. Here the sky was imagined as a watery lake (the cool waters of the stars) and so a boat was needed. It should be reasonable to assume that this scenario of boat riding over a body of water was based on the actual funerary process where the body of the deceased was transported from the east bank of the Nile over to the west bank, to be placed in the pyramid. That is why the last sentence indicates that the king shall be "at the fore of the westerners," that is, to rule over the kingdom of the dead in his new identity as Osiris, the Foremost of the Westerners (Khenty-Imenty).

Obviously, within just one account, the king's final destination was conceived as either in the sky or in the West, and he could be identified with Atum or Osiris. Such multiple or parallel views of the abode of the deceased king were in fact very common in the *Pyramid Texts* and other later religious texts such as the *Coffin Texts* and the *Book of the Dead*, which could have represented the

---

[12] *Pyramid Texts* (henceforth *PT*) Utterance, 213–14; Allen (2005: 31); Cf. Faulkner (1969: 40–1).

conciliation of different religious traditions or different religious discourses about the origin of the cosmos.

The text specifically warned the king to beware of the "lake"—which obviously was a dangerous place where the deceased were expected to encounter on his/her way to the world beyond. Other passages in the *Pyramid Texts* indicate that there were various kinds of lakes in the world beyond. Besides this "lake (of evildoers),"[13] there were "Lake of Life," "Lake of Osiris," Lake of the Jackal," "Lake of Cool Water," or simply "Lake of the Netherworld."[14] Obviously some of these lakes were beneficent: "You (Osiris=King) have come forth from the Lake of Life, having been cleansed in the Lake of Cool Water."[15]

In other spells, the king was identified with the Orion,[16] the place to be in the sky was a "Marsh of Reeds (or Field of Rushes)," where the deceased take a bath,[17] and the king was supposed to be ferried through a "Winding Waterway" to the eastern horizon.[18] As in early Greek belief, there was a "ferryman" who would ferry the king through the waterways.[19]

No matter where that destination of the deceased could have been, the Egyptian writers tried to fill in some descriptions of that world, including the journey that the deceased would have to take before reaching the final destination. Most frequently, a "Winding Waterway" was mentioned as the passage that the deceased have to take toward the destination.[20] Along the way, the deceased were likely to encounter any number of obstacles, including difficult terrains and malicious demons and enemies.

The malicious enemies included characters such as snake monsters[21] or apes who cut off heads[22] as the king declared to certain deities-guardians of the netherworld to prepare the way for him to pass through:

> O you in charge of hours, who precede the Sun, make way for Unis that Unis may pass within the circuit of Belligerent-Face.[23]

---

[13] According to the interpretation of Faulkner (1969: 177); *PT* Utterance 500, note 3.
[14] See index for "lake (š)" in Allen (2005: 458–9); Faulkner (1969: 327).
[15] *PT* Utterance 670; Faulkner (1969: 286).
[16] There are many other identifications of the king with various deities throughout the *Pyramid Texts*, which we shall not enumerate here.
[17] *PT* Utterance 325, 442, 563; Allen (2005: 68); Faulkner (1969: 104; 147–8; 218–19).
[18] *PT* Utterance 263, 473; Allen (2005: 48); Faulkner (1969: 72, 161).
[19] *PT* Utterance 475, 481, 516–22; Allen (2005: 128); Faulkner (1969: 163, 169, 190–6).
[20] For occurrences, see Allen (2005: 448); Faulkner (1969: 326).
[21] *PT* Utterance 226, 227, 233, 234, 240, 377–8; Allen (2005: 17–18, 88); Faulkner (1969: 53–7, 125).
[22] *PT* Utterance 254; Allen (2005: 44); Faulkner (1969: 64).
[23] *PT* Utterance 251; Allen (2005: 42); Faulkner (1969: 627).

Some of the seemingly dangerous places included the Island of Fire,[24] the Great Lake with striking power, and the Castle of the Mace of the Great Ones.[25]

On the other hand, there were many deities in this world of beyond that the deceased king could ask for help.[26] The deceased would also be supplied with the necessary nourishments in the new life to come: abundant food and drink so that there would be no need to worry about hunger and thirst[27] as the destination was also called "Field of Offerings."[28]

The *Pyramid Texts*, although basically a set of royal funerary ritual texts, should not be understood as merely "royal" and therefore having no wider social significance. The highly condensed and often poetic expressions employed in the *Pyramid Texts* marked clearly a very sophisticated intellectual stratum in society, as the texts must have been the culminated result of a long process of development. The rich religious and cosmological ideas contained in the texts could also only have been the sediment of a long religious tradition that was the manifestation of social and religious mentality. That they suddenly appeared in the Fifth Dynasty, though exact reasons are unknown, may again be understood as the result of the cumulative effect of the new beginning—new expressions in cosmological ideas and social ethics, and new designs of architecture that could match the new ideas—set forth by the Step Pyramid.[29]

Despite the seemingly congested or even confused presentation of various strains of imagination about the realm of postmortem existence for the king, we can sense a mentality or a strategy that tried to cull as much as possible what would be useful for the preservation and enhancement of the fate of the deceased in his/her next life. The uncertainty (to us of course) of the exact location of the destination is probably not because the Egyptians did not know the answer; on the contrary, it is most certain that when the *Pyramid Texts* were written, Egyptian religious speculation had already gone through a long development, and local traditions from different regions throughout the kingdom were probably employed at the royal funeral and finally preserved through the compilation of the *Pyramid Texts*. It is clear that the *Pyramid Texts*, though represented by versions from different pyramids, collectively constituted a genre of spells used in the royal funerals, with a high frequency of repetition and variation of some basic themes such as the resurrection of the king, the

---

[24] *PT* Utterance 249; Allen (2005: 42); Faulkner (1969: 61).
[25] *PT* Utterance 262. Allen (2005:47); Faulkner (1969: 71).
[26] For example, *PT* Utterance 301, 303, 304, 308; Allen (2005: 55–9); Faulkner (1969: 90–6).
[27] *PT* Utterance 338-49; Allen (2005: 74–5); Faulkner (1969: 109–12).
[28] *PT* Utterance 465; Allen (2005: 122); Faulkner (1969: 155).
[29] Poo (2022a).

identification of the king with certain deities, and the ascension to the sky. This all-encompassing and inclusive attitude toward different traditions was probably a way to show the supreme authority of the ruler. We shall see a similar situation in the Chinese case.

## The *Coffin Texts* and the *Book of the Dead*

However, the descriptions of the world beyond tend not to be too detailed in the *Pyramid Texts*. We are given the names of some locations and the deities or monsters awaiting there. What is happening, for example, in the Marsh of Reeds? We do not know. Interestingly, this question is to be answered in the *Coffin Texts* of the Middle Kingdom, the direct descendent of the *Pyramid Texts*, which is now being used by a wider population.[30] Thus people who could afford a decent coffin for their burial in the Middle Kingdom period would often have funerary spells inscribed on their coffins, employing phraseologies and religious allusions similar to those of the *Pyramid Texts*. The imagination of the world beyond, in particular, seems to have gained some degree of detail. For example, the Marsh of Reeds, or Field of Rushes, is described thus:

> I know that middle gate from which Re issues in the east; its south is in the Lake of Waterfowl, its north is in the Waters of Geese, in the place in which Re navigates by rowing or by wind. I am he who has charge of the rigging in the God's Bark, I am he who rows and does not tire in the Bark of Re; I know those two sycamores which are of turquoise between which Re goes forth, which go strewing shade at every eastern gate from which Re shines forth. I know that Field of Rushes which belongs to Re, the wall of whose enceinte is of iron; the height of its barley is four cubits, its ear is one cubit, its stalk is three cubits; its emmer is seven cubits, its ear is two cubits, its stalk is five cubits. It is the horizon-dwellers who reap it, 9 cubits only in the presence of the Souls of the Easterners, who are Harakhti, the ... calf and Morning Star.[31]

The text here gives a fairly idyllic image of the paradise-like world of the deceased, where there were giant barley and emmer, and the residents were called "horizon dwellers." Since we shall leave the subject of the source of such imagination to the next chapter, suffice it to say here that all the scenes described

---

[30] Faulkner (1980).
[31] *Coffin Texts* (henceforth *CT*) Spell 159; see Faulkner (1980, vol. I: 137–8).

in the text were aimed at expressing a central idea, that this was a better world compared with the one wherein the deceased used to live.

The netherworld, or at least part of it, was also often referred to as the Field of Offerings: "Acclamation is given to you in the realm of the dead by those who are in the Field of Offerings."[32] It was expected that, similar to the Field of Rushes, this was a paradise-like place where the deceased could enjoy endless happiness. The two were actually often mentioned together in the description of the netherworld: "I will live on bread in the Field of Offerings, I will have abundance in the Field of Rushes."[33] Whether the two fields were but different names for the same place, however, is probably not an issue in the context of a belief system that accepted a multiplicity of images regarding all kinds of possibilities in the realm of the deities and the netherworld.

This idea of the Field of Offerings persisted in the later era and was represented in the New Kingdom funerary texts such as the *Book of the Dead*.[34] One particular spell (*BD* 110) in the corpus of the *Book of the Dead* provided a rather interesting account of the deceased paddling his/her boat through the Field of Offerings. The spell begins with a long title:

> Beginning of the spells for the Field of Offerings, the spells for going forth by day, going in and out of the god's domain, attaining the Field of Rushes, existing in the Field of Offerings, the great settlement, lady of the winds, gaining control there, becoming a blessed one there, plowing there, reaping (there), eating there, drinking there, copulating there, doing everything that is done upon earth.[35]

It is evident that, simply by reading this title, the essential purpose of the *Book of the Dead* could be clearly understood: the deceased wished to have a life in the netherworld that could allow him/her to do everything that he/she used to do on earth. Whether or how this seemingly plain wish could have represented the kind of eternal happiness that the deceased were supposed to have in the netherworld, however, shall be discussed in the following chapters. The text continued to describe the place that the deceased were to venture into:

> N. (the deceased) shall say: Horus was seized by Seth. (But I) saw him who attacked against the Field of Offerings (Peace), and I freed Horus (from) Seth

---

[32] Faulkner (1980: 47).
[33] *CT* Spell 190, 216; Faulkner (1980: 158, 172).
[34] *Book of the Dead* is the name given to a group of funerary texts written on papyrus as part of burial equipment. The individual spells are referred to as *BD* xxx. See Faulkner (1985).
[35] Allen (1974: 87).

and opened the roads [of Re] on this [day] (when) the sky moaned [because of] Seth and the water [rose high] because Seth [was vexed] at the wind for its [bringing life to] him who was in (his) [egg] and rescuing him who was in the womb, (namely) Horus, from the Silent Ones.

Lo, I paddle (in) this great bark in the lake of Hotep (peace/offering); it is I who took it (i.e. the bark) from [the limbs] of Shu. (His) [limbs] and his stars are [years and seasons]. I paddled in her (i.e. the field's) lakes, so that I arrive at her settlements. I journey upstream to her Hotep, for I am [Hotep] in his [field].

I prevail over her (i.e., the field), (for) I am one who knows her. I paddle in her lake(s), so that I arrive at her settlements. My mouth becomes powerful, and I become sharper than the blessed. They shall not prevail over me. I provide for this they field, (O) Hotep, which thou lovest, they achievement, the [lady] of the winds. I become a blessed one therein; I eat (there)in, I drink therein. I plow therein, I reap therein, I grind therein. I copulate therein; my [magic] becomes powerful therein.[36]

It was by this time a common practice in the funerary texts that the deceased were identified with Osiris or other deities and participate in a variety of mythological stories. The principal myth was of course the Osiris cycle that included the contention between Horus and Seth.[37] A noticeable point was the pun on the word "offering" in the "Field of Offerings." As the Egyptian word for "offering," ḥtp, was etymologically the same as "peace," the "Field of Offerings" could also be read as "Field of Peace," probably referring to the final resting place of the deceased.

Thus, despite the "magical" nature of the texts—that is, they seemed to invoke certain supernatural forces at work and that there existed a plethora of deities that were often competing with each other or duplicating each other's functions—the entire funerary setup, including the funerary ritual procedures and the corresponding texts on the walls that indicated the sequence of the procedure, indicated a conscious and meticulous design that was based on a clear understanding of how the universe was structured, how the deceased could be revived and gain eternal life in that universe, and how protection could be rendered by the spells to ensure the safe journey of the deceased. This could not have been the product of a superstitious and prelogical mind. In other words, we need to appreciate the rationale that lies behind the funerary establishment,

[36] Allen (1974: 87).
[37] Griffith (1960).

beginning from the tomb construction itself, the evolution of the tomb style, the decoration of the walls, down to the funerary rituals, and the collection of the texts such as the *Pyramid Texts*, the *Coffin Texts*, and the *Book of the Dead*. These texts could be regarded as different versions of the same corpus of ritual texts that dominated and defined ancient Egyptian religion and the concept of the netherworld.

A most interesting point that could be deduced from a reading of the Egyptian funerary texts about the terrain of the netherworld is that whether in the *Pyramid Texts*, the *Coffin Texts*, or the *Book of the Dead*, all the movements and traveling of the deceased were done by boat and never on land. The texts constantly mentioned the deceased traveling by boat in the Winding Waterways, in the various lakes in the netherworld, or across the watery firmament in the sky. Rarely, if ever, do we see that the deceased traveled on land, except, of course, when the deceased's coffin was pulled over the sand toward the tomb. No donkey ride had ever been mentioned as part of the journey to the West, although in reality donkey rides would have been an ordinary way of transportation. This has to be interpreted as a product of the living reality of the Egyptian people, that travel on the Nile was considered synonymous with movement in general. The direction of traveling north, for example, is expressed by the word "going down stream" ($\underline{h}d$) with a boat sign. It is interesting to observe that the living environment of the Egyptians did put some constraint on their imagination of the netherworld, as hardly any natural phenomena outside of the Nile valley was part of that imagined land: hardly any high mountain, comparable to the Olympus in Greek mythology, was ever mentioned as part of the netherworld landscape, nor was the great Western desert. The marshland and the winding waterways seemed to suggest the complicated terrain of the Delta area and the marshes and sand dunes that often flanked the riverbanks—whereas no high mountains were mentioned as obstacles to be overcome in the journey to the Beautiful West.

There are certain descriptions of the netherworld that should be mentioned in addition to the most important Field of Offerings. For example, the texts mentioned certain buildings such as the halls of the officials (*BD* 147), the house of the gods (*BD* 146), the ten divine councils (*BD* 18), the seven chambers (*BD* 147), and the gatekeepers of the netherworld (*BD* 86). Thus, despite the predominating concern with the various challenges for the deceased, the Egyptians seemed to have also given some thought about the netherworld as a functioning bureaucracy.

## The Netherworld in Pre-Qin and Han Texts

The previous discussions of the changing tomb styles in early China from the vertical pit tomb to the horizontal brick tomb indicate that there should be a corresponding change of the ideas of the netherworld. In addition to the fact that the tomb style became more like a house for the deceased, the gradual change of funerary objects from ritual bronze vessels to objects of daily use, even model houses and rice paddies, indicated a shifting emphasis on the imagination of the netherworld; that is, from a world keen on preserving sociopolitical status to a world more interested in having a comfortable life. Moreover, there emerged a progressively realistic imagination of the netherworld in the sense that this netherworld began to be conceived with more and more details, mostly similar to those of the world of the living. In these respects, ancient Egyptian funerary objects were remarkably similar to those of the Han China, in terms of their imitation of the daily life.

Even so, there was no unifying conception of a netherworld in China. The earliest textual evidence from China concerning an idea of afterlife can be found in the Shang Dynasty oracle bone inscriptions. As is well-known, the oracle bone inscriptions were divination records of the Shang kings. Some of the inquiries were directed to the deceased kings who dwelt in heaven together with the Lord on High (Shangdi). Presumably this was a very special afterlife, available only to royalty. This situation was similar to ancient Egypt, where the kings were thought to have ascended to heaven in the company of the deities and among the stars. There was also no textual reference about the afterlife of the commoners, though burial custom continued to develop along the model of vertical pit style in various degrees of elaboration according to the status of the dead. This uniformed tomb style that spread across social strata implies that the belief system of the society at the time was by and large homogenous.

However, heaven was not the only destination of the deceased king. One inscription found on a Shang bronze vessel mentioned that the owner of the vessel, a loyal subject of the king, wished to be able to follow and serve the king "in the underground" after death.[38] This "underground," though without any elaborate description, must have been a common conception for the destination of the dead at that time. Human sacrifice and accompanying tombs of servants and concubines witnessed at the Shang royal tombs as well as certain later tombs and corroborated by textual evidence from the *Book of Odes*, attributed to the Zhou period, indicate that for a long time people believed that the deceased

---
[38] Zhang Zhenglang (1981).

kings and rulers needed the service of their servants after death. This would be an intuitive view of the netherworld, that is, it was where the deceased were buried together with his followers and his possessions.[39]

During the Eastern Zhou and the Warring States period (i.e., eighth to third century BCE), two terms—Yellow Spring and Dark City—were used to represent the netherworld. The term "Yellow Spring" was probably a reference to the underground water, used as a metaphor for the netherworld. The *Zuozhuan*, a historical record of the Eastern Zhou period, preserved a story that has to do with this concept of Yellow Spring. According to the story, the Duke Zhuang of the state of Zheng was angry with his unfaithful mother and vowed never to see her again in life. Later, when he regretted it, he dug an underground tunnel to meet with her so as not to break his vow. The expression used for the vow was: "We shall not see each other unless we all reach the Yellow Spring, (i.e., the netherworld)."[40] The underground tunnel was obviously seen as the substitute of a tomb or the netherworld. Exactly what was there in the Yellow Spring, however, was not specified in the existing evidence.

The term "Dark City (*youdu*)" first appears in the *Chuci* or *Songs of the South*, written by the famous Chu poet Qu Yuan (c. third century BCE). It was in the chapter entitled "Summoning the Soul," which describes the soul-recalling ritual, that the term "Dark City" appears:

> O soul, Go not down to the City of Darkness, where the Lord Earth lies, nine-coiled, with dreadful horns on his forehead, and a great humped back and bloody thumbs, pursuing men, swift-footed: Three eyes he has in his tiger's head, and his body is like a bull's.[41]

Here the Dark City was ruled by a Lord Earth (Tu Bo), a sinister-looking horned python. Such a description betrays a certain aversion toward afterlife, as the Dark City was obviously not a desirable place to be for the soul of the dead. Again, little was known about this Dark City. Indeed, darkness is a quality often attributed to the world of the dead. The ancient Mesopotamians believed that the world of the dead was a dark and cold place, ruled by the deities Ereshkigal and Nergal. The Jewish Sheol, also a dark place, was intimately related to the ancient Mesopotamian concept of the netherworld. The ancient Greek conception of the netherworld was also a gloomy place, where the souls of the dead existed in a pale and shadow-like form. The darkness of the netherworld, or the Dark

---

[39] Huang (1990).
[40] *Zuozhuan Zhengyi* (1976) 2: 20; Legge (1960), vol. V: 6. For details, see Poo (1998: 65).
[41] Hawkes (1959: 105).

City, was a concept retained well into the Eastern Han period. As an Eastern Han funerary text states: "(The deceased) joined the long night, without seeing the sun and the stars. His soul dwelled alone, returned down to the darkness."[42]

It is worthwhile noticing that, despite the lack of detailed information about the Dark City, at least the poet made a reference to an underground deity/demon, the horned python. One can therefore render some corroboration with the strange animals found in the Mawangdui T-shaped painting. Such imaginative animals or deities were not improbable in the minds of the people then. The *Song of South, Chuci,* it should be pointed out, originated from the Chu area, exactly where the Mawangdui tombs were located.

Exactly how prevalent this concept of a Dark City was in the late Warring States period when the *Song of South* was written, however, is uncertain. One finds, for example, the actual tomb itself could be the abode of the dead, as reflected in the early Qin Dynasty story of the resurrection of the person named Dan.[43] In the story, Dan—a retinue of an official by the name of Xiwu— committed suicide for fear of punishment because he had wounded someone in a fight, perhaps unintentionally. His body was exposed on the marketplace for three days before he was buried—obviously a kind of punishment for the crime that he had supposedly committed. Three years after his death, his former master Xiwu, for whatever reason, reopened the case and found that he (Dan) should not deserve death for his crime. Subsequently Xiwu reported to the Secretary of Controller of Fate (*siming shi* 司命史) by the name of Gongsun Qiang, probably an official who was responsible for the death sentence. Gongsun Qiang accepted the plea and had a white fox dig Dan out from his tomb. Four years later, he was able to hear the sound of dogs and chickens and was able to eat like an ordinary human being, though his limbs were still feeble.[44]

This extraordinary story provides a rare glimpse of the society, the legal system, the funerary custom, and the vivid imagination and literary expression of the people at the lower echelon of the government in the late Warring States period. But not the least of all, it provides us with a view of the idea of death and the netherworld.

Although no extensive information was given concerning the larger picture of the netherworld, the desire of the dead to lead a carefree life can be gleaned from Dan's statement on what was detested by the dead in the tomb:

---

[42] Nanyang shi bowuguan (1974).
[43] Li (1990); Harper (1994); Jiang (2013); Wu Wenling (2015).
[44] I follow the interpretation of Wu (2015).

Dan says: "The dead do not want many clothes. The dead think that white woolly-grass makes one rich, and the ghosts think it is more precious than other things." Dan says, "Let those who offer sacrifices at tombs not dare to cry. If they cry, the ghosts will depart and flee in fright. If people consume the food immediately after the sacrifice, the ghosts will be offended and not eat again." Dan says: "Those who offer sacrifices must carefully sweep and purify. Do not wash the place of sacrifice with dirty water. Do not pour the boiled dish over the sacrificial food, for the ghosts will not eat it."[45]

According to the account, the dead still possessed senses of their own. As Dan recounted, the dead or ghosts did not like to put on clothes, and they would detest greatly those who came to the tomb to make offerings yet for the real purpose of eating the food. One can vividly imagine such a scene by the grave side. The ghosts would also like their grave site be cleaned carefully. People should not pour broth over the offering because ghosts would not eat it. This interesting anecdote about the life of the dead in the tomb was an example of how people could have imagined the netherworld, although only a glimpse of it. Similar ideas about resurrection after three years, the preference of ghosts regarding clothes, and the proper behavior of food offering ritual by the tomb were also found in another text, now preserved at Beijing University.[46]

In comparison, the Egyptian dead seemed to have expected something even worse, as sentences such as "I will not rot" or "I will not eat feces" in the netherworld appear quite often in the *Coffin Text* and the *Book of the Dead*.[47] Apparently these were among the obstacles that the Egyptian dead would have to encounter in the netherworld. The difference is that the story of Dan relates how the living people had caused trouble for the ghosts, while the Egyptian dead were confronting bad fate in the netherworld. Moreover, the Egyptian dead would cast curses on those who would do harm to the tomb, while the Chinese ghosts only complained about the ill-treatment by the living.

There was no attempt at presenting a general picture of the netherworld. Presumably, since the soul/ghost of each dead person stayed in the tomb, the netherworld would consist of all the tombs and their occupants. Suggestions have also been made, based on a late Warring States period incantation text for the dead soldiers, that the dead will go to a place called Mount Buzhou.[48] The

---

[45] Li (1990); Jiang (2013). The text is full of philological problems; my translation consults several different studies and basically follows Jiang (2013).
[46] Li (2012); Jiang (2014).
[47] *Coffin Texts* Spell 432 (not rot), 173 (not eating feces), *Book of the Dead* Spell 45 (not rot).
[48] Lai (2015, chapter 5).

purpose of the text was to call for the safe return to the home of the ghosts with the help of a deity named Wu Yi. This text expands a little our knowledge of the terrain of the netherworld of the Warring States period. It also hints at the possibility of traveling in the netherworld from one place (Mount Buzhou) to another.

Just as the living people needed to travel for various reasons in this world and expected to get back home safely, there is no inherent conflict between the idea of the tomb as the home of the deceased (therefore the tomb needs to be supplied with all sorts of objects, not only for travel but also for daily use) and the idea that the deceased sometimes also need to travel. In the "resurrection story" mentioned earlier, the deceased Dan stayed in his tomb all the time and enjoyed (or endured) the offerings of family members for three years. There was no sign of his going anywhere. The tomb as a "home" for the dead, if conceived metaphorically, must also be conceived as having the function of a home in the way the living would have. That is, the home should be a base to carry out a person's livelihood, as the person works in the field, goes to the market, and travels afar for business but always comes back. For the home should be a person's resting place, whether in life or in death.

In the Western Han, in the second century BCE, texts found in tombs referred to the world of the dead as simply "underground" (*dixia*) and managed by a host of bureaucrats, including "Lord of Underworld," "Assistant Magistrate of the Underworld," "Assistant of the Dead," "Retinue of the Graves," "Minister and Magistrate of Grave Mounds," "Commander of Ordinance for the Mounds," "Neighborhood Head of the Gate of the Souls," "Police of the Grave Mounds," "the Marquis of the Eastern Mound," "Count of the Western Mound," "Official of Underneath," and "Head of Five of Gaoli (netherworld)."[49] Above this rather complicated bureaucratic establishment, there was an overlord, variously known as the Yellow Emperor (Huangdi), Yellow God (Huangshen), or Heavenly Emperor (Tiandi). It is unclear how the Heavenly Emperor would be involved in the affairs of the netherworld if the heaven and underground were separate regions. Yet given the heavenly bodies and deities presented in the Mawangdui and other early Western Han paintings, the two regions were not necessarily unconnected.

For example, a group of wooden slips found in Hunan province and dated to 79 CE provided some interesting information on the rituals performed in connection with death and burial.[50] The texts were written in the form of

---

[49] See Poo (1998, chapter 7).
[50] Chen Songchang (2001).

a contract in which it was recorded that when a person was about to die, the family members would employ a *wu*-shaman to pray and make ale and meat offering for him/her. When the person died, the family members would pray again to a variety of deities, including the Lord Hearth, the Controller of Fate, and a number of local deities. Sacrifice to the deities was also ministered by local *wu*-shamans. When the prayer was finished, the content of the prayer and the offering were then written on wooden or bamboo slips, to be taken by the deceased as a kind of contract to the Heavenly Sire (*tiangong*), to testify that indeed prayers and offerings had been performed on behalf of the deceased. It is unclear who this Heavenly Sire was, though he must have been one of the important deities in charge of the deceased. This, of course, is another form of the bureaucratization of the afterworld, as official documents on earth were imitated in the world of the dead. It is particularly interesting that here the deceased were referred to as ascending to heaven and descending to the Yellow Spring at the same time when death occurred.

The fact that the underground world was staffed by officials reflects the situation above ground. Because of the increasing importance of written documents in the development of a centralized government, people's conception of the netherworld was also affected. In other words, a concept of bureaucratic netherworld was only possible when the world of the living was already bureaucratized. The evidence from the Han might not have reflected the beginning of this bureaucratization of the netherworld, since texts from the Warring States period had already suggested this trend. The correspondence addressed to the underworld bureaucracy represented by the deity Wu Yi, mentioned earlier, attests to this new frontier of imagination. In this new imagination, the government of the living needs to communicate with the government of the dead, thus forming a continuum of bureaucracy from life to death.[51] The Han documents make it certain that this underground bureaucracy has all the signs of part of a unified empire.

One of the most revealing documents on the bureaucratization of the netherworld was a type of text, the so-called tomb quelling text, found in Eastern Han tombs. Here is an example:

> Today is an auspicious day. It is for no other reason but the deceased Zhang Shujing, who unfortunately died prematurely, is scheduled to descend into the grave. The Yellow God, who produced the Five Mountains, is in charge of the

---

[51] Lai (2015, chapter 4).

roster of the deceased, recalling the *hun* and *po*, and in charge of the list of the dead. The living may build a high tower; the dead returns and is buried deeply underneath. Eyebrows and beards having fallen, they drop and became dirt and dust. Now therefore I (the Messenger of Heavenly Emperor) present the medicine for removing poll-tax and corvée conscription, so that the descendants will not die. Nine pieces of ginseng (*renshen* 人參) from Shangdang substitute for the living. The lead-man (*qianren*) is intended to substitute for the dead. The soybeans and melon-seeds are for the dead to pay for the taxation underneath. Hereby I issue a decree to remove the earthly evil, so that no disaster will occur. When this decree arrives, restrict the officer of the Underworld, and do not disturb the Zhang family again. Doubly urgent as prescribed by the laws and ordinances.[52]

The first half of the text relates how the dead were managed by the Yellow God, as the messenger of the Heavenly Emperor presented various offerings to help the living descendants as well as for the benefit of the deceased. Presumably, the spell could have the magical power to transform the soybeans and melon seeds into the payment for taxes in the netherworld. Moreover, there was also the fate of forced labor waiting for him. The lead man, actually a small lead figurine, crudely made and put in a clay bottle to be buried in the tomb, was said to be able to do all sorts of errands, including serving as corvée labor to substitute for the deceased. It is interesting to note a similarity between this lead figurine and the ushabti (or shawabty) of ancient Egypt: both served as substitution of the deceased for conscription labor in the afterlife. Spells written on the Ushabti also engaged the "double" to answer (which is the literal meaning of "ushabti") for all the required works.[53] We shall return to this in the next chapter. Most interestingly, the Messenger of the Heavenly Emperor, presumably the person who wrote the text, had the power to issue a decree to remove the earthly wrongdoings and restrain the netherworld officials from disturbing the family members of the deceased, so that there would be no more death in the family. In this small circle of bureaucracy, therefore, when the proper gifts (offerings/payments) were made, the local official (i.e., the Messenger of Heavenly Emperor) could wield certain power to help the deceased and his/her family.

Sometime during the late Western Han or early Eastern Han, a number of new localities emerged as the final destinations of the deceased. The most important was Mount Tai, the ancient sacred mountain on which the emperor ascended

---

[52] Poo (1998: 171–2).
[53] See Poo (2003). See Chapter 5.

to make sacrifice to the heaven in order to implore for blessings.[54] It became the gathering place of the souls of the dead and was ruled by a certain Lord of Mount Tai. This does not mean that the belief in an underground netherworld or the Yellow Spring was entirely replaced by the Lord of Mount Tai or that people in every corner of the empire would give up their local traditions. The process through which Mount Tai gained its importance is obscure, but it might have to do with the position of Mount Tai in the state cult. The *Shujing* or *Book of History* mentions that the Sage-king Shun once made a sacrifice at Mount Tai. Another ancient tradition is that the Yellow Emperor performed a sacrifice to heaven at Mount Tai and became an immortal. A number of classical texts testified that the mountain deities were worshiped by the rulers in order to appropriate the mandate of heaven, therefore the legitimacy to rule. The First Emperor of Qin and Emperor Wu of Han also performed the Grand Ceremony (*fengshan*) at Mount Tai. The sacred nature of Mount Tai was therefore well established during the early Han. One can only assume that the sacredness of Mount Tai was the basis for it to become the abode of the dead. Nonetheless, it is only in the Eastern Han period that we find some funerary texts that clearly indicated that Mount Tai had already become the abode of the ghosts. One such text reads: "The living belong to the jurisdiction of Changan to the west; the dead belong to the jurisdiction of Mount Tai to the east."[55] This indicates that the capital of the living was Changan, the capital of Western Han, which indicates that the concept was probably formed during the Western Han period, and the capital of the dead was Mount Tai. Thus it seems that it was during the Western Han that Mount Tai gained the attribute of being the abode of the dead, although in fact the text was found in an Eastern Han tomb. Two small mounds below Mount Tai, Liangfu and Gaoli, also became associated with this world of the dead and were often mentioned in texts of Eastern Han and later eras. As it is not clear what was there in Gaoli or Liangfu, we know more about Mount Tai. The idea that Mount Tai was the place where the netherworld was located was graphically described in a story about a certain Cai Zhi:

> Cai Zhi was the county clerk of Linzi. Once he was delivering a message to the governor and suddenly lost his way. He arrived at Mount Tai, and saw something like a city wall, so he went in and delivered the message. He saw an official with the guards and paraphernalia like a governor, who then set up a feast for him. At the end, the governor gave him a letter, saying: "You shall deliver this letter to

---

[54] Yu (1987); Liu (1997).
[55] Zhang Xunliao and Bai Bin (2006).

my grandson." Cai answered: "Who is Your Honor's grandson?" "I am the god of Mount Tai. My grandson is the Heavenly Emperor." The clerk thus realized that what he had reached was not in the human world.[56]

Literary imagination of the netherworld as a bureaucracy in the period after the fall of the Han Dynasty was even more developed than what was described in the Han funerary texts. The communication between the living and the dead was very much at the center of such type of stories. A famous story quoted in the following about a certain Jiang Ji relates how his dead son appeared to his wife in a dream and demanded to be assigned to a more comfortable position in the netherworld bureaucracy. The way to do it, according to the son, was for Jiang Ji to find a person who, as the son revealed, was about to die and to be appointed as the Magistrate of Mount Tai in the netherworld bureaucracy and would have the authority to reassign a good position for his son. Jiang acted according to the plan, and indeed sometime later his son appeared in his dream again and said that he got a new and better position.[57]

Jiang Ji was the general, one day his wife dreamt about their deceased son, who cried in tears and said: "How the living and the dead go different ways! When I was alive I was the heir of high officials. Now I am in the Underground and serve as the conscript soldier of Mount Tai, and I am extremely distressed and humiliated beyond words. Now a person named Sun Ah who lives to the west of the grand temple has been summoned to be the Magistrate of Mount Tai. I wish mother could tell father to ask Ah and transfer me to a comfortable position." When he finished, the mother awoke suddenly. Next day she told Jiang Ji about it, Ji said: "it was merely a dream, there is nothing strange about it." The next night, [the son] again came to the mother's dream:

"I come to accompany the new lord [Sun Ah] and stayed by the temple. Because there is time before setting out, so I find a moment to come home. The new lord should set out at noon tomorrow. There will be many errands to attend to, and I shall not be back. I am hereby to say farewell. Because father's *qi* was strong and could not be affected [in his dream], I therefore appeal to mother, and wish you talk to father again, why not just try it." The son then described the feature of Sun Ah in detail. The next day, the mother again told Jiang Ji, "Although there is nothing strange about a dream, but this is too extraordinary, why not just give it a try." Jiang Ji thus sent some one to the grand temple and inquire about Sun Ah and indeed found him, and his feature was exactly as the son described. Ji cried

---

[56] Lu Xun (1986: 145).
[57] Lu Xun (1986: 139–40).

in tears and said: "I almost let my son down!" He then went to see Sun Ah and told him about the matter. Ah did not fear that he should die but on the contrary glad to become the magistrate of Mount Tai, and he only worried about whether Jiang Ji was telling the truth. Sun said: "If it happens as your honor says, it is my wish. I wonder what kind of position your son wishes to have?" Ji replied, "Give him whatever that is comfortable in the Underground." Ah said, "I will surely follow your command!" He then gave Ji a rich reward, and sent him back. As Ji wished to know whether the prediction will be proven true, he had people lined up every ten paces from his office to the temple so as to learn the news about Ah quickly. At the hour of *chen* (8 am) it was said that Ah had a heart pain. At the hour of *si* (10 am), it was said that Ah's pain became severe. At noon, the death of Ah was known. Jiang Ji cried and said: "Although I mourned about my son's misfortune, it is nevertheless a happy thing that the dead had senses." After a month or so, the son came to the mother's dream and said: "I have already been transferred to become a secretary." [58]

Many other stories involve the communication between the living and the dead or the underground officials. Since the world of the dead permeated the world of the living, communication between the two was often the linchpin that allowed the stories to develop, such as stories about a person coming back from death, a person called to death by the netherworld officials, or a person visited by netherworld officials for businesses.[59]

During the fourth and fifth centuries, when Buddhism and Daoism rose as competing religions in China, many stories revealed the rivalry between the Daoist and the Buddhist for their efficacy of dealing with the marauding ghosts.[60] In the meantime, the story was also framed in the bureaucratic context of this world and the world after death, and the two were basically identical.[61]

## Comparative Note

The Egyptian imagination of the netherworld as described in the funerary texts shows that the netherworld contains bodies of water, river, Field of Rushes, Island of Fire, and above all the Field of Offerings where the deceased are supposed to spend eternity. Numerous deities and demons were mentioned as

---

[58] Lu Xun (1986: 139–40).
[59] Lu Xun (1986: 94, 145, 156, 158, 159, 160, 215–7, 258, 259, 297).
[60] See Poo (2022, chapters 5 and 6).
[61] Lu Xun (1986: 181–2).

what the deceased would encounter along the journey, as either helpers or foes to the deceased. The deceased, on the other hand, culled together with spells and actions of all the help he/she could manage, identifying him/herself with various deities, to fight for the promised life in the land of Osiris. That the netherworld was also a bureaucracy, albeit a divine bureaucracy, was made abundantly clear by the *Book of Dead*'s spell 125—the judgment of the dead. The dead had to go through a series of procedures: weighing the heart by Anubis, the result of the weighing recorded by Thot, and judged by Osiris. To enter the forty-two gates was another symbolic procedure to show the complex bureaucracy that characterizes most governments.

With the goal finally achieved, the deceased were to live a carefree life in the Field of Offerings, as described in the *Book of Dead* spell 110:

> Beginning of the spells for the Field of Offerings, the spells for going forth by day, going in and out of the god's domain, attaining the Field of Rushes, existing in the Field of Offerings, the great settlement, lady of the winds, gaining control there, becoming a blessed one there, plowing there, reaping (there), eating there, drinking there, copulating there, doing everything that is done upon earth.[62]

Plowing, reaping, eating, drinking, and copulating were the foremost activities that the deceased wished to do in paradise, the Field of Offerings. Perhaps this was just what a perfectly relaxed life should be.

As for China, in so far as the funerary texts are concerned, the most frequently mentioned items were the various underground personnel, beginning with the highest Heavenly Emperor or Yellow God down to the local bailiff. Thus this netherworld bureaucracy seemed be more detailed than the Egyptian description of the netherworld bureaucracy. The difference is obvious: the Egyptian netherworld as described in the funerary texts was a place in action; that is, the deceased were to go through a series of challenges, tests, and threats, in order to reach the destination. It was full of drama, tension, and anxiety. In the Chinese netherworld, if we take the face value of the funerary texts, the deceased seemed to go through a normal transition from one bureaucracy (of the living) to another (of the dead). For example, a funerary text was cast in the form of bureaucratic transaction of personnel:

> On the thirteenth year, the fifth month, day of Gengchen, the Assistant Magistrate of Jiangling dares to tell the Assistant Magistrate of the Underworld that the *wufu* (conscript soldier) of Shiyang, Sui Shaoyan, and the slave Liang

---

[62] Allen (2005: 87).

and others, a total of twenty-eight persons, .... And four riding horses, can be used to serve. I hereby dare to report to the Lord.[63]

The deceased Sui Shaoyan and his slaves were reporting to the Underground Assistant Magistrate, just as he would have done when he moved to another district while on earth. This small detail tells a lot about the imagination of the Han people about the situation in the netherworld. There was no drama waiting to happen or unexpected deterrence from any deities or demons. Life after death seemed to be a continuation of life on earth.

Yet the more interesting thing is the details of this imagined community: What kind of activities are mentioned and why? The cursory account above of the extent Chinese textual evidence shows that the aspects most frequently touched upon are some functions of the underground bureaucracy, such as the collecting of taxes, the conscription of corveé, and activities of the underground local officials, such as reporting about the coming of new residents; that is, the newly dead.[64] It would be quite intuitive for us to surmise that they reflected conceptual imitations of the institutions of the human world. Presumably, before the development of the more complicated government structure, say before the formation of the Qin–Han bureaucracy, it would hardly be possible for such a concept of underground bureaucracy to take shape. Yet the fact that the activities mentioned in the texts were limited to only a few items indicates that the nature of the texts was a bureaucratic one: it was only meant to deal with the specific problems for the dead. It should therefore not be seen as representing the entire view of the netherworld during the time. The most obvious evidence to corroborate this observation is the graphic source that we have discussed in the last chapter. It can be stated that most of the tomb paintings and reliefs of the Han period, whether they were about daily activities or special auspicious signs, were depictions of a carefree and prosperous life. In so far as they could also be interpreted as reflecting the kind of happy life that was anticipated in the netherworld, the emphasis was obviously different from what we see in the tomb-quelling/exorcistic texts. Nonetheless, the emphasis on certain bureaucratic measures in these texts undeniably indicates a prevailing trend to envision the netherworld as mainly a bureaucracy to be dealt with. If this could be seen as a reflection of the most pressing concern of the living, it says something about the deeply ingrained apprehension of the overwhelming control of the state machine in the life of the common people.

---

[63] Jinancheng Fenghuangshan 168 hao Hanmu fajue zhenglizu (1975).
[64] Zhang Xunliao and Bai Bin (2006: 285).

Turning back to Egypt, it is also obvious that the tomb paintings preserved a snapshot of a happy life for the deceased, which did not reflect the content of the funerary texts. Except, as we already mentioned, that if we take the tomb paintings as a description of an ideal life, either on earth or in the netherworld, as depicted in the *Book of the Dead* Spell 110, then there is a meeting point between the paintings and the texts. The tomb paintings, taken as a whole, could be seen as representing life in the Field of Offerings. Except perhaps copulating, the paintings have depicted the activities mentioned in the *Book of the Dead* Spell 110: plowing, reaping, eating, drinking, and everything that is done on earth.

5

# Belief, Ethics, and the Life Hereafter

Social ethics is not necessarily an explicit component or final goal of religious belief, not necessarily the embodiment of the teaching of a higher being that is geared toward a salvation or a good life in the hereafter. However, it could be an implicit social contract developed during the growth and evolution of a society. Only by following certain consensus or rules of behavior can a society survive and grow in a viable and sustainable fashion. Religious belief adds a layer of support for this social ethics by providing a more explicit contract between humans and gods or extra-human powers. Thus the Egyptians found Maat as the ultimate and ever correct principle that guides social behavior.[1] In this sense, Maat is close to the Chinese term "*dao*" (literally "way" or "path"), the correct and just principle of the universe. The negative confession in chapter 125 of the *Book of the Dead*, for example, though cast in the context of last judgment before Osiris, was no less a set of totally secular social ethics, guaranteed or upheld not only by the deity/Maat, but also by the king, who is the final arbiter of human relations. Yet an even deeper authority not often mentioned was the social convention. The authority of the king derives from this social convention and religious tenets reinforce it, to the extent that its ultimate origin—that is, the society itself—was often neglected.

The Egyptian hereafter, according to the view of Jan Assmann, is a moral institution.[2] The basic idea is that the setup of the entire concept of the netherworld was constructed explicitly on the premises that only a morally perfect person can have the qualification to be in the netherworld. This is not the case in China, as we shall discuss in the following.

At the outset, however, it should be noted that we as modern researchers need to avoid reconstructing a world—either the Egyptian or the Chinese—according to our wish of how a better society should have been. For example, when we

---

[1] Lichtheim (1992, 1997); Assmann (2002: 127–31).
[2] Assmann (2002: 157–9).

compare the Egyptian Judgment of the Dead with Christian Last Judgment and say that both were referring to a supreme god who upheld a moral standard to judge the dead and decide who should be granted access to the kingdom of God or the Beautiful West, it sounds perfectly reasonable and natural to an ear that is familiar with the Christian idea, but it is certainly not a necessary condition for every society, including that of the Chinese.

## Egyptian Social Ethics and Beliefs in the Afterlife

From the graphic description of the netherworld, this chapter turns to the more abstract aspects of ethical values and social behavior that could have informed visions of the netherworld. For example, in many Egyptian biographical inscriptions, there are some typical expressions that announce the virtue of the deceased:

> I am son to the aged, father to the child, protector of the poor in every place. I have fed the hungry, anointed the unkempt, I have given clothing to the naked.[3]

> O you who live on earth, soul priests of the estate of my lord, as my lord favors you every day, you shall give bread, beer, and water, the reversionary offerings of my lord. I am one of you, a speaker of perfection and a repeater of perfection. I never said anything evil against anyone, I never seized anything from any poor man. With regard to any man who shall make invocation offerings for me—no matter whether a brother, a son, any person, a scribe—and who shall pass by this tomb and who shall read (the inscription on) this doorway, I shall be his support in the court of the Great God. I am an excellent and true lector priest. The *imakhu* in the sight of his lord, the royal noble, the companion of the house, Bia.[4]

The invocation for people who shall pass by the tomb to make offerings was made on the grounds that the deceased claimed that he was morally just and was sanctioned by the Great God and honored also by the king. On the other hand, anyone who shall do harm to the tomb shall be brought to justice by the deceased in front of the god, presumably after death:

> And as for any people who will do something badly to this, who will do something destructive to this, who will erase writing from it, the judgment of

---

[3] Lichtheim (1997: 20).
[4] Sturdwick (2005: 269).

my case about it with them will be by the great god, lord of judgment, in the place where judgment is (held).⁵

The recognition that worldly unjust could be rectified by the power of the gods was not only revealed by the threat formulae in these "appeals to the living" and the "letter to the dead" discussed in the last chapter, but it was also articulated into a set of positive social and ethical values that people regarded as prerequisite for one to enter the blessed land of the Lord of the Netherworld. In Old Kingdom tombs, we often encounter expressions similar to the following:

> I came forth from my town, I went down into the afterlife;
> I carried out Maat for her lord,
> I propitiated the god in accordance with what he desires;
> I said what was perfect and repeated what was perfect;
> I spoke and acted truly;
> I gave bread to the hungry, and clothes to the naked;
> I was respectful of my father and kind to my mother as far as I was able;
> I never said anything evil, unjust or devious against any man,
> Through desire of being happy and to have clear character,
> And that I may be *imakhu* in the sight of the god and of men forever.⁶

In some of the more articulated biographies, the personal virtue received extensive elaboration. Such examples include the inscription in the tomb of Akhethotep/Hemi and Nebkauhor (Fifth to Sixth Dynasty):

> The beloved one of the king, Osiris, Anubis and Khentyimentyu is any inspector of soul priests, assistant inspector (of soul priests), scribe of a phyle, or (ordinary) soul priest of my funerary estate who carries out the rites in accordance with these instructions which I have made while was alive and on my feet.
>
> For I am one who speaks, I am one who acts, I am one who is remembered … by many people. I never spent the night [in the state of anger] … his majesty. With regard to any man with whom I was angry, or who did something which irritated me or (did) something hateful, I it was myself who pacified him. With regard to any man about whom I knew that they were locked up in the Great Mansion, or were beaten in the Great Mansion, or were punished on guard duty, I did not … I never blocked any path, I never went above traveling by foot or by boat, I never did what any of his rivals loved, I never excused the evil of another (man) in the presence of his majesty, I never made any command or any will in any place except for.⁷

---

⁵ *Urk.* I: 70, 15–71.
⁶ Strudwick (2005: 278).
⁷ Sturdwick (2005: 262).

The deceased was portrayed as a person of integrity, who did not vent his emotion against his opponent and who did not do unjust things but only the right ones. The emphasis that he was a person remembered by many people indicates the importance of social consensus, that a person needs to be accepted by his peers. In the end, the king's approval was a defining qualification for him to pass on to a blessed afterlife.

An even more elaborated statement details the kind of personal virtue that was probably held as a high standard at the time is the biographical text of Ankhmeryremeryptah of the Sixth Dynasty period:

> Never did I beat any man there so that he fell as a result of my action; never did I enslave anyone therein. With regard to anyone therein with whom I dealt, I am he who propitiated them; I never slept in a state of anger with anyone. I it was who gave clothing, bread, and beer to everyone who was naked and hungry there. I am the beloved one of everyone; I never said anything evil against any man to a king of someone in power. I am one favored of father and mother and of the noble ones in the necropolis for making invocation offerings for them.[8]

This kind, compassionate, just, and filial person who is now in the necropolis could also be a person depended upon by his fellow citizens to seek help on behalf of them before the Great God.

These expressions certainly portrayed an idealized image of the deceased. Yet the fact that they were part of the biographical texts indicates that they represented a certain ideal ethical value that was the consensus of the society, an ideal that qualified a person to pass into the blessed world of the dead in the land of the god Osiris. It is important to note that the society had now developed a mature, self-critical, and self-conscious ethical system that was in harmony with its religious belief. This ethical system demonstrated a clear reflection on how a proper social relation should be conducted, not unlike the Confucian social ethics in its fundamental aspects, which to be sure was not to say everyone in society would necessarily abide by such an ideal. China before Buddhism was a body of more or less coherent cultural entity, with prevailing intellectual and religious traditions, albeit encompassing different branches of thought and practices and a rich variety of customs that nonetheless coexisted within this body of tradition.

Moreover, the fact that such expressions were often included in the biographical texts also suggests that there was a certain conscious effort to propagate such an

---

[8] Sturdwick (2005: 267–9).

ideal, perhaps through scribal education system and disseminated among the elites in society, for it was only the elites who could have the means to own a proper tomb with inscriptions and decorative paintings. This is clearly indicated in the biography of Ankhmeryremeryptah quoted previously: "Since you wish that I intercede on your behalf in the necropolis, then *teach your children* the words of making invocation offerings for me on the day of my passing there" (emphasis added).

The most often mentioned ethical values from the Old Kingdom period, in view of the abovementioned discussion, could be summarized in several points: first, the emphasis on good relationships with people in general, regardless of relative positions, from one's superior, parents, and friends to the general public, especially the "poor" people—compassion and fairness were always the stressed virtues; second, maintain a relationship with the gods, follow Maat, and be confident of having the support of the gods. Apparently, the Egyptians took their social relationships and roles very seriously, so that the fulfillment of the social and religious obligations was the condition leading to the claim that the person was an *imakhu*, a perfectly blessed soul, qualified to live in the Land of Osiris.

Such ethical values might have been the source of the belief in the judgment of the dead in later eras, as similar ethical principles appeared in the form of negative confessions in the *Book of the Dead* chapter 125. The famous "negative confessions" in this text listed all sorts of wrong behaviors that were opposite to the social standard. If we read it in a reversed way, this text could be seen as a sort of "handbook for good behavior" for average Egyptians who wished to be admitted into the Land of Osiris:

> Hail to you, great God, Lord of the Two Truths!
> Lo, I come before you,
> Bringing Maat to you,
> Having repelled evil for you.
>
> I have not done crimes against people,
> I have not mistreated cattle,
> I have not sinned in the Place of Truth,
> I have not known what should not be known,
> I have not done any harm,
> I did not begin a day by exacting more than my due,
> My name did not reach the bark of the mighty ruler,
> I have not blasphemed a god,
> I have not robbed the poor,

I have not done what the god abhors,
I have not maligned a servant to his master,
I have not caused pain,
I have not caused tears,
I have not killed,
I have not ordered to kill,
I have not made anyone suffer,
I have not damaged the offerings in the temples,
I have not stolen the cases of the dead,
I have not copulated nor defiled myself,
I have not increased more reduced the measure,
I have not diminished the arura,
I have not cheated in the fields,
I have not added to the weight of the balance,
I have not falsified the plummet of the scales,
I have not taken milk from the mouth of children,
I have not deprived cattle of their pasture,
I have not snared birds in the reeds of the gods,
I have not caught fish in their ponds,
I have not held back water in its season,
I have not dammed a flowing stream,
I have not quenched a needed fire,
I have not neglected the days of meat offerings,
I have not detained cattle belonging to the god,
I have not stopped a god in his procession.

I am pure, I am pure, I am pure, I am pure.[9]

We quote this entire list because it is important to know what was the general perception of a system of social ethics that could maintain the smooth function of society. This includes not only interpersonal relationships or social etiquettes, such as how to treat people and how to behave righteously, but also some religious matters. It is interesting that the religious matters are of two kinds: those related to the attitude toward the god—"not blasphemed a god" and "sinned in the Place of Truth"—and those related to the temple properties—"snared birds in the reeds of the gods" or "detained cattle belonging to the god"—which could be seen as part of the economic activities, because the temple properties were not free for anyone to take. Most of these items are concrete descriptions of behaviors—even

---

[9] Lichtheim (1976: 124–6).

"blasphemed a god" is relatively clear—yet the sentence "sinned in the Place of Truth" implies a certain abstract idea of ethics or religious piety. On the whole, the negative confession of the dead needs to be approved by Osiris during the judgment, as the heart of the deceased was weighed against Maat, the Truth.[10] The Egyptians, by using the concrete picture of the scale, expressed an abstract idea; that is, when the heart is of the same weight as the Truth, which means the person is free of any moral flaw. Similarly, although it may seem somewhat random to list those concrete and individual items seemingly without any logical system, these behaviors can be seen, like the heart on the scale, as concrete symbols of the abstract principle, the Maat. These behavioral codes, therefore, are the keys and foundation for the Egyptians to enter into the world of Osiris.[11]

In the long history of ancient Egypt, it has often been reminded that there must have been changes in the intellectual development that could have affected the social values. However, hard evidence does not come easily. Lichtheim has observed certain changes in the individual expressions in the biographies and argued that the moral consciousness of the Egyptians in the Old Kingdom emphasized that to do the correct things approved by society was an achievement worth mentioning in one's life story, while in the Middle Kingdom and the New Kingdom, the emphasis switched to the inner quality of a person; that is, "what I am" is even more important than "what I do."[12] Judging from the negative confession in the *Book of the Dead* chapter 125, however, we can still see that "what one does" is overwhelmingly more important—that is, mentioned many more times—than "what one is." Perhaps the distinction is really not necessarily that important in the Egyptian case, because one can argue that "what one is" is the reason or motivation for one to do "what one does." In other words, the distinction between "what one does" and "what one is" seems to be a modern take based on the assumption that the inner quality of a person is more desirable or truthful than the outward behavior, an assumption that ultimately derived from Judeo-Christian tradition, whereas in the Egyptian tradition, to do the right things would be sufficient proof of an upright character.

In order to support this observation, we shall go through the Egyptian literary texts that are most relevant to ethical values, namely the so-called wisdom literature or didactic literature, and examine the connection between social value and religious piety.[13] As early as in the *Maximum of Ptahhotep*, an

---

[10] Lichtheim (1992).
[11] Lichtheim (1997).
[12] Lichtheim (1997: 22).
[13] An extensive discussion of "wisdom" could be found in Lichtheim (1997).

ideal personality was portrayed as the following: He is modest, reticent, and obedient to social hierarchy. He is a content, reserved, and good-tempered person, who always maintains a good relationship with people of all levels of status; those above, equal, and below him are all treated politely and with respect and consideration. The actions and human skills are moreover under the scrutiny of the gods, as "people's schemes do not prevail, god's command is what prevails."[14] It can be observed that Ptahhotep was obsessed with the human skill, a distillation of years of experience as an official and an elder who had seen many people and experienced the vicissitudes of life. The text also reveals to us the character of the society that produced such a kind of social ethics.

This "program" of building an ideal social persona was echoed in the *Instruction of Prince Hardjedef* as a self-reliant, modest, and content person, who takes care of his family and heir and who also recognizes that in the end a person needs to realize the flimsiness of human life, "given that death humbles us, given that life exalts us, the house of death is for life."[15] In the *Instruction Addressed to Kagemni*, again, modesty, silence, and contentedness were advocated, with the warning that "one knows not what may happen, what god does when he punishes."[16]

In the pre-Middle Kingdom text *The Instruction Addressed to King Merikare*, in addition to some advice that obviously is the concerns of a ruler, such as to guard the borders and secure the forts, the king was given advice appropriate for a good local official like Ptahhotep: Giving good speeches and treating the neighbors and people in the town amiably and fairly.[17] And despite the fact that the advice was given to the king, who theoretically was the god himself, the advice was nevertheless cast under the watchful eyes of the god: "While generation succeeds generation, god who knows characters is hidden. Once cannot oppose the lord of the hand, he reaches all that the eyes can see."[18] This clearly shows that the composition of this text was firmly rooted in a scribal tradition of didactic literature, as individual composition might have been catered to each specific situation, and the basic tenet was more or less followed throughout the centuries: be good and fear the god.

The Middle Kingdom text in the tomb of Paheri continues the Old Kingdom tradition but added something new. The text provides a rather elaborate description of life beyond, about having a tomb, taking a place in the realm of

---

[14] Lichtheim (1975: 63).
[15] Lichtheim (1975: 58).
[16] Lichtheim (1975: 60).
[17] Lichtheim (1975: 101).
[18] Lichtheim (1975: 105).

Osiris, becoming a living *ba*, having bread, water, and air, and every faculty of the body in good functioning state, very much in the spirit of the *Coffin Texts* and the *Book of the Dead*.[19]

The effect of the accumulated repertoire of ethical values is that the articulation of ethical behaviors became more sophisticated, with layers of experiences and intellectual exercise over all sorts of interhuman and human–divine relations. Gods, however, were always there in the discourses expressed in the wisdom literature. Furthermore, it was probably during the New Kingdom that a new twist emerged regarding human–divine relations; that is, the acknowledgment that god's will cannot be predicted.

In the *Instruction of Any*, dated to the early New Kingdom, the author advocated a modest, just, and independent person who handles social relations well, takes care of family and friends, and is pious toward the gods. However, the author also expressed certain doubt that if the course of life could be smooth: "Furnish your station in the valley, the grave that shall conceal your corpse, … Do not say 'I am young to be taken,' for you do not know your death."[20] This uncertainty of one's fate continued in the *Instruction of Amenemope*, dated to the Ramesside period. Here the ideal personality, a modest, content, all-round kind and well-behaved person, was extolled as before. Yet amidst the positive tone, the firm advice about a secured path to a comfortable life, there were grains of doubt about the validity of human efforts:

> The words men say are one thing,
> The deeds of the god are another.
> Do not say: "I have done no wrong,"
> And then strain to seek a quarrel;
> The wrong belongs to the god.[21]

There is no guarantee of divine approval of human actions, of all the seemingly good intention that men strived to maintain. Thus the author repeatedly says, "Indeed you do not know the plans of god, and should not weep for tomorrow; settle in the arms of the god, your silence will overthrow them (i.e. the opponents)." The optimistic mood found in the earlier instructions, such as in *Ptahhotep* that if one strives to be good one will succeed, is now replaced by uncertainty. Therefore there is more reason to suspend expectation, "not weep for tomorrow," and give oneself in to the mercy of gods.

---

[19] Lichtheim (1976: 15–21).
[20] Lichtheim (1976: 138).
[21] Lichtheim (1976: 157).

It has been argued that the Akhenaten religious revolution, wherein the sun god Aten was promoted to be the omnipotent divine power, basically de-emphasized the netherworld and death. As a result, the traditional social morality and meaning of life that were dependent upon the belief in a future life in the netherworld lost their anchor.[22] This loss of meaning was reversed with the death of Akhenaten and the return of the traditional belief system, and the expression of this revival of the idea of the protection by the netherworld can be seen in the increasing emphasis on scenes of the netherworld in the private tombs since the Ramesside period, in contrasts to the more this-worldly life experience that was displayed in the Eighteenth Dynasty tombs.[23]

We apparently could not find exact correlations between the changing of moods in the tomb paintings and the wisdom literature. Yet it seems that a trend of turning inward, a realization that god's will cannot be predicted, was clearly present in the texts. This realization led to the development of the so-called personal piety, a more urgent need to have access to and receive blessings directly from the gods, which Egyptologists have been discussing for some time.

Yet the realization of the god's unpredictability was perhaps not new, since the unpredictability of god's will was probably part of the foundation of religious beliefs. That is to say, the divine power was never a single-purpose power with the welfare of human beings always in mind. There needs to be certain built-in uncertainty regarding the reliability of the gods, so that the believers are always kept at a certain level of suspension to wait for the favors and blessings of the gods, with a cloud of doom hanging in the back of their mind.

Traces of this more skeptical view about how much human beings could rely on the help of the divine beings could be detected from some unexpected contexts. For example, regarding the very common "appeals to the living" of the Old Kingdom period discussed earlier, the usual explanation is to read the appeals as they are: asking the passers-by to give offerings and prayers, and threatening to avenge those who did not respect or shall damage the tomb. However, these words could also be understood to be arising due to anxiety, distrust, and a sense of uncertainty about the fate of the dead in the tomb, despite all the good deeds that the dead claimed that he/she had performed in life.

For another example, in the "Harper's Songs" that appeared since the First Intermediate Period, the urge or advice of the author to his audience to enjoy

---

[22] Baines (1991).
[23] Assmann (1995: 66); Meskell (1999).

happy days while alive betrays a fundamental disillusion about the Western paradise:

> Those who built tomb,
> Their places are gone,
> What has become of them?
> ....
> Their walls have crumbled,
> Their places are gone,
> As though they had never been/
> None comes from there,
> To tell of their state,
> To tell of their needs,
> To calm our hearts,
> Until we go where they have gone!
>
> Hence rejoice in your heart,
> Forgetfulness profits you,
> Follow your heart as long as you live!
> Put myrrh on your head,
> Dress in fine linen,
> Anoint yourself with oils fit for a god.[24]

Since god's blessing could not be guaranteed, one should simply enjoy what a god would enjoy. It would be perfectly reasonable, therefore, to read the Harper's Songs as a type of didactic literature, to teach the living how to understand the meaning or meaninglessness of life, and to find a best solution to worldly sorrow and doubt.

This strand of skepticism, as argued earlier, lasted till the end of Egyptian history. In the Demotic didactic text contained in the Papyrus Insinger, we found the traditional advice that a wise man should be pious and modest and follow the principle of Maat, echoing what *Ptahhotep* and *Any* had said before. The added touch of the unpredictability of god's will, of the fact that those who lived according to the principles of good citizenship may still find themselves devastated by bad luck and became poor, while those who did not care about the teachings of gods were rewarded with good fortune, could indicate a more sophisticated understanding of the distinction between faith and reality.[25] Yet it is also important to note that the theme of the reverse of fortune—the good become poor and the evil become rich—was a familiar one, already voiced in

---

[24] Lichtheim (1975: 196–7).
[25] Lichtheim (1980: 184–5).

texts such the "Admonitions of Ipuwer" or "Dispute between a Man and His Ba." Thus one should probably not say that this was a late development of the Egyptian intellectual horizon and the depth of their religious consciousness. This side of the Egyptian psyche, which led to the struggle between hope and fear, and the prospect of a happy netherworld, shall be further developed in the next chapter.

## Chinese Ethical Values Related to the Idea of the Netherworld

In the last chapter we have mentioned the story on the resurrection of a person named Dan. In the story, Dan gave a statement about his own experience in the grave and complained about the behavior of the people, perhaps even including his own family members who came to the graveyard to make offerings with rather sloppy manners by discarding leftover food over the grave. This statement provides a glimpse of the ethical values connected with death and justice. First of all, the story was built upon the idea that the netherworld bureaucracy could make mistakes that should and could be corrected. According to the narrative, the office of the Controller of Fate apparently allowed an unjust mistake—the suicide of Dan—to happen. It was therefore the good fortune of Dan to be brought back to life when the Controller of Fate corrected the mistake. This points to an important feature in the development of the vision of the netherworld in the later eras. As I have argued elsewhere, the ghost stories that circulated in society ever since the time of the Spring and Autumn periods represented by the *Zuozhuan* present us with a netherworld that often needs to be rectified of some injustice.[26] This is inherently a skeptical attitude toward the world, human or divine. It is an indictment of the imperfectness of the human world and a distrust of the divine order.

Secondly, Dan's complaint also hints at a social convention that was probably becoming an issue. It has to do with the behavior of the people who made offerings at the grave side and who were not respectful toward the deceased in the tomb. The messy "table manners" of the tomb visitors described by Dan was apparently a negative example of the prevailing good social behavior. The Egyptians made similar observations in the appeals to the living about the possibility that the tomb could be desecrated, but they also posed threats to those who should do

---

[26] Poo (2004); Poo (2022b).

harm to the tomb and thus to the deceased. There did not seem to be any curses by the Chinese dead against those who should desecrate the tomb.

When we come to the Han period, references to the netherworld from the writings of the intellectuals are categorically different from what can be deduced from the funerary objects and the funerary texts, mainly the "tomb quelling texts" and the like. This division manifested itself in the different attitudes regarding the issue of lavish/thrifty burial. The intellectuals who were inclined to the Confucian ethics in general held the view that it was unnecessary to provide excessive funerary objects for the dead, but they were not against certain appropriate funeral as an expression of filial piety. The two opposing positions were presented dramatically by the story of a certain Yang Wangsun (fl. mid-second century BCE), who was apparently a Daoist follower. When Yang was about to die, he left his will to his son:

> I wish to be buried naked so that I may return to my true home. You must not go against my wishes! When I am dead, put my corpse in a hemp bag, dig a hole in the ground seven feet deep, and lower me into it. Then take hold of the bag at the end where my feet are and pull it off so that my body will rest directly on the ground.[27]

Yang's idea was radical enough at the time, but he was not the first to have such an idea. The early Han philosophical work *Huainanzi* (淮南子) had a sober view of life and death:

> When I am alive I have a seven-foot body; when I died I have a coffin full of soil. Comparing my life with those of the beings with physical bodies, is just like my mingling with the formless after my death. And yet my life will not add to the number of things in the world, my death will not add to the thickness of the earth. How would I know which of the two should I prefer more than the other?[28]

This idea, in turn, was a direct descendant of the view of the Warring States Daoist philosopher Zhuangzi. According to the book of *Zhuangzi*, when he was about to die, his disciples planned to have a lavish funeral for him. But Zhaungzi turned down the offer:

> I have the heaven and earth as my coffin, the sun and moon for my ornaments, and the stars and planets as pearls to fill my mouth, I have all these things around

---

[27] *Hanshu* 67: 2907; trans. Watson (1974: 107–9).
[28] *Huainanzi* (1971; 7: 4a).

as my funeral gifts; don't you think these are ample? And what can be added to them for my funeral?²⁹

Thus the netherworld was denied. Death is the end of a person, but the world remains the same. This Daoist view, though still shockingly strong even today, was conceivably a weak rebuttal of the prevailing custom of lavish burial of the author's time. Nor did Yang Wangsun receive support from his friends and family members. A friend of his by the name of Marquis Qi heard about his decision and wrote a message to him:

> I have heard some talk of your leaving orders to be buried naked. If the dead have no consciousness, then that will be the end of the matter. But if they do, I'm afraid you will be subjecting your corpse to humiliation in the world below. Do you intend to appear naked in front of your ancestors? Personally I don't think you should do so. Moreover, the Classic of Filial Piety says: "Let clothes, coverlets, and inner and outer coffins be provided for the dead," and these after all represent the rules handed down from the sages. Why must you alone be different and insist upon following some private learning of your own? I hope you will give careful thought to the matter.³⁰

Marquis Qi's view was probably that of a typical Confucian who did not have a firm view of things regarding ghosts and spirits or life hereafter. Yet they would not deny outright the possible existence of a netherworld, thus the need to consider what a proper burial would be. The debate was extensive, with a central idea quoted in the Confucian *Analect*: "When the parents are alive, serve them according to the propriety (*li*); when they are dead, bury them according to the propriety; and make offerings to them according to the propriety."³¹ But could it imply that the dead still possessed certain senses and certain need for offerings? This can be interpreted differently. For those who believed that there was a life beyond, offerings are necessary. But for those who did not believe there was a netherworld, the funerary rituals are still important, to show people that the society needed to have a proper *li*—ethical values and standards of behavior—to show necessary respect for the departed. The main argument was that a proper funeral was not only a show of respect for the departed, but by showing the respect it was also a confirmation of the existing social order, regardless of whether the netherworld really existed or not.

---

²⁹ *Zhuangzi jishi* (1985: 1063).
³⁰ *Hanshu* 67: 2907–8, trans. Watson (1974: 107–9).
³¹ *Lunyu zhushu* (1976; 2: 2b).

This view, even if it did not wholeheartedly admit that there was a netherworld where the dead would reside and therefore consume the offerings, had opened a door for the continuous practice of lavish burial, simply because it was difficult to draw a line between the "appropriate" and the "excessive" ways of the funerary arrangement.[32]

Although Yang Wangsun's view was too radical to be followed by his contemporaries, his idea at least influenced a continuous strand of intellectuals of the Han Dynasty and later generations. According to my study, there were at least nineteen intellectuals in the Han Dynasty who expressed in one way or another their wish to have a thrifty burial.[33] Most of them were educated in Confucian classics, some with interests in Daoism or divination, and all of them served in government in certain capacities. The fact that these intellectuals continued to express ideas about how people should practice a modest or thrifty style of burial indicates that the vast majority of the people in society, including those with Confucian persuasions, continued to supply their tombs with luxury items as far as they could. Thus we hear about cases where funerary objects were stacked up by rich merchants for profit:

> The rich people of Maoling by the names of Jiao and Jia spent tens of millions of coins to stack up secretly those funerary equipment such as charcoal and weeds. When Emperor Zhao died, the funerary setup was suddenly in demand, the officials could not acquire the necessary equipment. Yiannian submitted that "Certain merchants had previously bought up the funerary equipment, in the hope that when a sudden need arises, they could make a profit. This is not what a subject should do. They should be confiscated by the government."[34]

While this happened in the capital area under the surveillance of the court officials and the extortion of funerary objects involved even the royal funeral, we could surmise that other places would have more similar problems. A story about a certain official's activities tells how he persuaded the local people to abandon the custom of lavish burial and adopt proper, presumably more prudent, rituals, with the effect that those who sold funerary objects went out of business and had to discard the funerary objects on the street.[35] Again, the fact that the story made an impression on the historian indicates that the overall social convention was probably exactly to the contrary.

---

[32] Poo (1990); Poo (1993, chapter 8).
[33] Poo (1993, chapter 8).
[34] *Hanshu*, p. 3665.
[35] *Hanshu*, p. 3210.

This conflict between the official attitude and the common people's view toward burial indicates a struggle between political-moral authority and prevailing social ethics and common sentiments, which we do not find in Egypt. It seems that the Chinese society had a strong autonomous view not easily persuaded by official ideology regarding what was appropriate in funeral arrangements. This in turn implies a different view of the netherworld held by the commoners regarding the existence of the netherworld and what it meant to the people. The official attitude, under the influence of Confucian ethics, advised people to be prudent, if not the kind of thrifty burial advocated by Yang Wangsun and his followers, in funerary matters. But it did not provide a clear position about the existence of the netherworld; thus, the persuasion was never totally effective. The consequence of this imbalanced situation—that is, the lack of a clear position about the netherworld and the fate of the dead on the side of the official elites and the commonly accepted idea about the netherworld and the need of the ghosts of the deceased on the side of the majority of people in society—was the continuing practice of lavish burial throughout the country.

As the Confucian scholar said in the *Discourse on Salt and Iron* (*Yantielun*):

> In ancient times people served the living with love, and buried the dead with grief; therefore, the sage made rules and ceremonies not as empty formalities. Nowadays people cannot respect the living; [they only vie with each other] in the luxurious gifts [displayed in the funeral] when [their parents] die. Although no sorrow or grief is expressed, as long as rich burial and abundant funerary goods are furnished, it is called filial piety. His name will be known to the world, his fame remembered by the fold. So the people all emulate and follow this kind of example, even to the extent of selling their houses and properties [to furnish the funeral].[36]

*Yantielun* was a collection of court debate in the reign of Emperor Wu of Han between officials who advocated the development of commerce and industry and state monopoly of salt and iron production on the one side, and Confucian scholars who favored more conservative way of governing and opposed to state monopoly and promotion of commerce and industry on the other. Here in this quote, the Confucian scholar, following the main stream of Confucian thought, was worried about the extravagant custom of peer competition for showing off one's wealth, instead of expressing genuine remorse for the loss of one's kinsfolk.

---

[36] Huan Kuan (1992: Book 6, p. 6).

In searching for an explanation for the necessity of the funerary objects, an assumption about the need of the dead seems to be straightforward. The ideal life in the netherworld, in this context, would be very much material-oriented: abundant objects of all sorts for making up a good and comfortable living. The situation has been summed up vividly by Wang Chong (20–98 CE):

> Thus ordinary people, on the one hand, have these very doubtful arguments (about whether ghosts exist or not), and on the other … note that the dead in their tombs arise and have intercourse with sick people whose end is near. They then believe in this, and imagine that the dead are like the living. They commiserate with them, [thinking] that in their graves they are lonely, that their souls are solitary and without companions, that their tombs and mounds are closed and devoid of grain and other things. Therefore they make dummies to serve the corpses in their coffins, and fill the latter with eatables, to gratify the spirits. This custom has become so inveterate, and has gone to such lengths, that very often people will ruin their families and use up all their property for the coffins of the dead.[37]

Wang Chong points out that people thought it was for the benefit of the dead that the funerary equipment was supplied, for they could not bear to see their kinsfolk spend their time in the netherworld with insufficient supply.

Thus the view that the netherworld was a place similar to this world was the persisting reason for the transferring of this-worldly values to the next. These values include material possessions and ethical principles. What was deemed desirable in life must also be supplied for the deceased in the netherworld. The Han intellectuals who tried to confront and amend this prevailing social norm could hardly be said to be successful in getting their ideas across to the public, even though their arguments were based upon a modest view of accommodating the need of the deceased in the tombs.

## Comparative Note

The above discussion has shown that social values are integral to the envisaging of a world after death. An interesting example for comparison in this regard, which we have hinted at in the previous chapter, can be found in the Egyptian funerary statuettes called ushabti and the Chinese funerary figurines called

---

[37] Wang Chong (1990: 461). For translation, see Forke (1962: 369).

the "lead man (*qianren* 鉛人)." Both were designed to serve as the "double" of the deceased in the netherworld whenever they were called upon to perform manual labor.

The Egyptian ushabti figurines are usually in the form of a standing mummy. On the figurine was usually written a standardized spell, which was part of the *Book of the Dead*:

> Ye ushabtiu, if N. is counted off, (if N. is assigned) to any work that is wont to be done yonder in the god's domain (lo, obstacles have been set up for him yonder) as a man to his duties, to cultivate the fields, to irrigate the shores, to transport sand of the east to the west, "I will do (it); here am I," shall ye say.[38]

It may seem somewhat extraordinary that the Egyptians should have thought that the dead were still subjected to hard labor even in the netherworld. The blessed world of the dead was not entirely free of anxieties after all. Yet seen from a comparative perspective, this idea was probably not as extraordinary as one might have thought in the first place. As just mentioned, the lead man, found in a number of Eastern Han tombs, was usually placed inside a clay bottle, with inscriptions on the bottle, such as the following:

> Use the lead-man to substitute for oneself. The lead-man is versatile, he can grind grain and cook, and he can drive a carriage and write letters.[39]

Apparently, after proper magical spells had been cast on them, these figurines were considered as substitutes for the deceased to perform certain duties that were required of the dead in the netherworld. Contrary to the surrogate statuettes of servants often found among the funerary equipment, they were not meant to serve the deceased, but as the double of the dead to substitute them when they were called to do work in the netherworld. The similarity between the ushabti and the lead figurine may seem striking. The use of other funerary objects such as servant figurines and sundry objects of daily use, as well as tomb paintings,[40] moreover, may strengthen the impression that both the Egyptian and Chinese funerary customs bear similar assumptions about the netherworld; that is, the netherworld was essentially the reproduction of the world of the living. Everything in this world was therefore expected to happen in the next

---

[38] Allen (1974: 150i). For specimens of ushabti, see Saleh and Sourouzian (1986, nos. 150, 151, 172, 182).
[39] Ikeda On (1981: 270, no. 2).
[40] Wang (1982).

world, with the exception that the deceased, with the help of the magic ushabti and the lead figurine, could escape from the expected hard labor.

Thus the relationship between social values and the vision of the netherworld was clearly demonstrated by these statuettes. This, however, does not mean that the two religious systems were similar in their funerary beliefs, but, on the contrary, points to a new window for studying both in a more critical way: What kind of religious and sociocultural system could have produced such objects? What was the social status of the owner of such artifacts and what was their significance?

To pursue further the cultural and religious contexts of the Chinese lead figurines, we found that the figurines and the clay bottles that contain these figurines always featured very crude material and workmanship, which means that the owner did not spend too much fortune in preparing them. Moreover, since the tomb owners had the apprehension of being summoned to work in the netherworld as servants or corvée labors, it seems to suggest that they were not of high social status. It is tempting, therefore, to suggest that the owners of these figurines were of relatively low social status. But how low? If we look at the archaeological reports about the tombs in which these lead figurines were found, the tombs and what remained in the tombs were decent enough to be ranked among the average "middle-size" tombs.[41] Thus there is no reason to say that the user of the lead figurines was of a low social status. The fact that they can afford to have a tomb already places them on a certain propertied level in society. Of course, none of the tombs wherein such lead figurines were found were more than average size. Another point worth noticing is that among thousands of Han Dynasty tombs discovered, only very few contained the lead figurines, indicating that it was perhaps not a prevailing custom. In any case, we can only tentatively suggest that the users of the lead figurines were not among the elites.

By contrast, tombs of the very rich, like those of the royal family and nobility represented by the Mawangdui tombs, contain surrogate figurines of servants and all sorts of household utensils that were designed for the service and use of the tomb owner, but no lead figurine was ever found. When we consider this level of evidence, the similarity between the lead figurine and the ushabti begins to take a new level of meaning. While the lead figurines were associated with the lower-middle class, the ushabtis were found mostly in the tombs of people with certain amount of wealth. The use of ushabtis was not an indication of the low

---

[41] Poo (1993).

social status but, on the contrary, a demonstration of the relatively high social and economic status of the user in the sense that the tomb owner could afford to supply the ushabtis. It was, moreover, a reflection of the peculiar idea that hard labor was waiting for the deceased in the netherworld, regardless of his/her social status on earth. One is reminded of the extraordinary horde of ushabtis found in the tomb of King Tutankhamun. Thus, despite the hope of passing the judgment of Osiris and dwelling in the Beautiful West, the possible conscription to perform hard labor remains a grim prospect of the fate of the deceased. This idea indicates that the Egyptian netherworld was after all not entirely based on the world of the living. The rich and powerful in Chinese society, on the other hand, never seemed to have to worry about a hard life waiting for them in the netherworld. This, I hasten to add, applies only to China before the inroad of Buddhism from the third and fourth centuries onward, since the Buddhist idea of postmortem punishment in hell began to change the perception of the relationship between one's moral behavior in life and the lot that one receives after death. This connection between morality and postmortem punishment, in the case of Egypt, also implies that one's social and economic status on earth does not guarantee a similar life thereafter.

It is through this more comprehensive comparison that we began to see that, although on the surface the ushabti and the lead figurine served similar functions in the conceptual construction of the fate of the dead—that is, they all served to substitute the dead to perform certain services in the netherworld—a comparison of the contexts of their origin and relative importance in each religious tradition opened up a new understanding of the idea of the netherworld in both Egypt and China. The assertion that the idea of the netherworld, either in China or in Egypt, was modeled solely after the world of the living appears crude in light of the comparison. It seems that, for the ancient Chinese, life in the world after death was basically what one could make of it. For the relatively well-off, abundant funerary equipment could ensure a comfortable life hereafter. For the relatively poor people, measures were taken to guard against possible misfortune in the netherworld. The use of lead figurine was one, and the use of magic to convert beans and melon seeds into money to pay taxes in the netherworld was another example.[42] In other words, the wealthy would not worry about what they did not suffer while alive, and their funerary equipment guaranteed a well-provided life after death. The less fortunate, however, would fear that what they had suffered while on earth would strike them again after death, thus the use of

---

[42] Poo (1998: 171–2).

the lead figurines and the beans and melon seeds. This seems to indicate that the Chinese way of using the lead figurine was closely connected with the social and economic status of the deceased. Because of the lack of postmortem judgment and an idea of a general fate for all, the rich had no need of the lead figurines.

In contrast, for the Egyptians, the concept was that all the dead, be they king, noble, or commoner, suffered a similar fate and were answerable to hard labor in the netherworld. In light of the use of the Chinese lead figurine, which seems to suggest that it was a reflection of both the anxiety and the social status of the deceased, the use of ushabti in Egypt seems to be both an indication of the belief in the postmortem judgment and a guarantor of avoiding hard labor, as well as a demonstration of the wealth and status of the deceased. Since hard labor was the expected fate of all of the deceased, those with means could supply themselves with ushabtis; the richer they were, the better and the more ushabtis would be supplied.

The practice of burial was such an ingrained element in society that very few in the ancient times could have thoroughly reflected upon the implications of the funeral. In China, the prevailing social ethics demanded a funeral for the dead, which implies a recognition of the existence of the netherworld, whether or not most people had given any thought about it. This recognition implies that the dead could exist in a certain form in the netherworld and would need certain sustenance to survive. People of different social status, however, had different imaginations of the need or the life of the dead according to their status, and this status was measured not by the "personal quality"—that is, whether the person was a "good and moral" person when alive—but by the material wealth that one or one's family could supply. This is demonstrated by our discussion of the Chinese "lead man." Thus the Chinese social ethics related to the imagination of the netherworld was mainly concerned with the propriety of the funeral: How a funeral, including all the burial ceremony and paraphernalia, should follow a certain *li*-propriety had been the concern of most people in society. That is to say, people were concerned with the ritual conditions for a person to enter into the netherworld, but these ritual conditions were not related to the person's inner quality. In Wang Chong's comment on the contemporary funerary custom, quoted above, there was no indication that a person's moral character had anything to do with whether the person could have a comfortable life in the netherworld.

For the Egyptians, on the other hand, the membership in the netherworld was conditioned by people's moral behavior, as reflected by the social ethics connected with the judgment after death. Unlike China, where a pronounced system of proper burial, as recorded in the *Book of Rites* (Chapter 2), was propagated by the Confucian school of thought—regardless of whether the system was followed in reality—the Egyptians did not seem to have any regulation regarding the "excessiveness" of the burial. Their ethical concern was not on the degree of extravagance of the burial, but on the moral integrity of the deceased. This is why the deceased would declare him/herself as an "*Imakhu*"—a morally justified and blessed spirit—because only an *Imakhu* is qualified to enter the Land of Osiris.

# 6

# Hope, Fear, and the Quest for Happiness

If the functions of any religion could be summed up, they would likely be the provision of hope, the eradication of fear, and the attainment of happiness. These are ultimately connected to what was viewed as the fate of a person after death. While the material conditions that may define what could be hoped for, what should be feared, and what constitutes happiness might not necessarily have been different across cultures, the manifestations of these concepts certainly could be very different. Consequently, we shall examine the expressions that the ancient Chinese and the Egyptians employed in their quest for happiness in connection with their construction of the netherworld. The genres of Egyptian texts such as the wisdom texts, biographies, letters, poems, as well as all the religious texts bear witness to an understanding of the assumptions regarding an ideal state of existence or happiness. Various Chinese texts and inscriptions discovered in the tombs expressed assorted views of the prospect and preparation for a life after death. They also provide evidence of hope for a better life to come or measures to remove fear and uncertainty. The fulfillment of the tasks that these texts set out to perform, either to ward off malicious spirits or to attain a comfortably settled life in the hereafter, betrays the idea of happiness that people held when preparing the funeral. It is important, moreover, that we should trace as far as we can the social background of the concept of the netherworld so that our discussion of the relationship between it and the daily experience of the people as well as their idea of happiness could be grounded in a firm historical context. Finally, we shall seek to explain the reasons why similar social and material conditions could have produced different expressions and what such differences reveal concerning the character of each of the parties in question.

## Hope, Fear, and Happiness in Ancient Egypt

The Harper's Song in the Middle Kingdom tomb of a person named Iki reads as follows:

> O Tomb, you were built for festivity,
> You were founded for happiness!
> The singer Neferhotep, born of Henu.[1]

It is a rather poetic expression in a positive tone describing the function of a tomb. Instead of saying the tomb is a house of eternity, here the tomb is founded for happiness. But can we really say that this is a departure from the tradition of seeing death and life in the netherworld as somehow a happier version of life on earth when the dead would receive all kinds of good offerings and be with the gods in the Field of Offering? Probably not. Yet it should also not be surprising that there were certain skeptical views about all the establishments of worldly fame and wealth as well as the promised Land of Osiris as but illusions. The by now famous Harper's Song gave a sober observation of the house of eternity, the tomb:

> He is happy, this good prince!
> Death is a kindly fate.
> A generation passes,
> Another stays,
> Since the time of the ancestors.
> The gods who were before rest in their tombs,
> Blessed nobles too are buried in their tombs.
> (Yet) those who built tombs,
> Their places are gone,
> What has become of them?
> I have heard the words of Imhotep and Hardedef,
> Whose sayings are recited whole.
> What of their places?
> Their walls have crumbled,
> Their places are gone,
> As though they had never been![2]

Thus even the house of eternity could not withstand the erosion of time. In a country that was filled with numerous ancient tombs and their ruins, the scene

---

[1] Lichtheim (1975: 194).
[2] Lichtheim (1975: 196).

would be a daily reminder of the flimsiness of human endeavor to an observant person, let alone the Harpers, whose job was singing at the funeral banquets, thus in a particular position to have witnessed many dramas of mourning moments and bereavements. As the beginning of the song says: "Song which is in the tomb of king Intef, the justified, in front of the singer with the harp." This is a hard-nosed look at the reality of what time does to human beings. The singer continues with a disillusioned statement about the unknowable netherworld, an agnostic attitude that recognized the absolute separation between this world and the netherworld.

> None comes from there,
> To tell of their state,
> To tell of their needs,
> To calm our hearts,
> Until we go where they have gone!
> Hence rejoice in your heart!
> Forgetfulness profits you,
> Follow your heart as long as you live!
> Put myrrh on your head,
> Dress in fine linen,
> Anoint yourself with oils fit for a god.
> Heap up your joys,
> Let your heart not sink!
> Follow your heart and your happiness,
> Do your things on earth as your heart commands!
> When there comes to you that day of mourning,
> The Weary-hearted hears not their mourning,
> Wailing saves no man from the pit!
> Refrain: Make holiday,
> Do not weary of it!
> Lo, none is allowed to take his goods with him,
> Lo, none who departs comes back again![3]

The solution to the hard fact that the famed Land of Osiris might never be reached was to make merry, if one could, with one's time on earth. Studies of similar songs have raised the question of whether or not such songs were really "hedonistic," abandoning belief and ethics and seeking only temporary pleasure. Since it is difficult to establish a fixed pattern of such kind of Harper's songs, it

---

[3] Lichtheim (1975: 196–7).

is perhaps best to treat the individual songs as representing a single voice and analyze accordingly.[4] For the song quoted earlier, the skepticism is unmistakable and rightfully occupied a special position in the intellectual history of Egypt, where conformity to tradition was the overwhelming moral behavior.

According to the predominant tradition about the netherworld, then, worldly desires were to be satisfied in the Field of Offerings, for food offering was a major concern in the funerary texts. One of the spells of the *Coffin Texts* even made a special emphasis "not to eat faeces and not to drink urine in the realm of the dead," for it was expected that only food fitful for the gods would be given to the deceased.[5] The fear or even the thought of eating feces and drinking urine in the netherworld, nevertheless, must have been an ingrained repulsive reaction to an unpleasant imagination of what was waiting for the deceased.

In the "letter to the dead"—already mentioned in the previous chapter—a person could write to his/her deceased kinsfolk and ask for help. For example, in the following letter, a man wrote to his deceased father:

> This is an oral reminder of that which I said to thee in reference to myself: "Thou knowest that Idu said in reference to his son: 'As to whatever there may be yonder (?), I will not allow him to be afflicted of any affliction'. Do thou unto me the like thereof!" Behold now there is brought (to thee) this vessel in respect of which thy mother is to make litigation. It were agreeable that thou shouldst support her. Cause now that there be born to me a healthy male child. Thou art an excellent Spirit. And behold, as for those two, the serving-maids who have caused Seny to be afflicted, (namely) Nefertjentet and Itjai, confound (?) them, and destroy for me every affliction which is (directed) against my wife; for thou knowest that I have need thereof (?). Destroy it utterly! As thou livest for me, the Great one shall praise thee, and the face of the Great God shall be glad over thee; he shall give thee pure bread with his two hands. Additional remark: Moreover I beg a second healthy male child for thy daughter.[6]

The writer first asked his father to help him produce a son and then he asked the father to help his wife Seny to get rid of the affliction caused by their two maids. He then asked the father to help his—the father's—daughter, therefore the writer's sister, to have a second son. In return, the son hoped that the Great God would bless the father in the netherworld and provide him with pure bread. The text was written on the surface of a clay bottle and presumably put in the tomb

---

[4] Lichtheim (1975: 194–6).
[5] Faulkner (1980: 147–8; 154–8).
[6] Gardiner and Sethe (1928).

chapel as a communication to the dead. It shows that the Egyptians believed that a written message, perhaps after the performance of certain ritual with magic effect, could be sent to the deceased and that the deceased somehow had the power to perform certain tasks to protect his or her descendants, including warding off bad luck, dispelling misfortune, and to bless the descendants with offspring. All these were humble hopes that ordinary Egyptians would like to be fulfilled by their kinsfolk in the netherworld. The fact that the letter was written on a crude clay bottle indicates the relatively low social status of the person and the family. Similar situations could be found in some Han Dynasty tombs, as magical spells and incantations were written on crude clay bottles and buried with the dead as protection.

In another letter, the writer hoped that the deceased could be taken care of by the goddess Hathor and at the same time have the power to ward against hostilities that the family members of the author were suffering from. It was also hoped that the deceased could appeal to a netherworld court for justice upon earth. It apparently acknowledged that the deities in the netherworld court could also be responsible for matters on earth:

> O Mereri, born of Merti! Osiris-Khentamente makes for thee millions of years by giving thee breath into thy nose, by giving thee bread and beer at the side of Hathor, the Lady of the horizon. Thy condition is like (that of one) who lives a million times by order of the gods who are in heaven and on earth. Thou makest obstacle to the enemies, male and female, of evil intent against your house, against thy brother, and against thy mother who … for her excellent son Merer(i). (As) thou wast excellent on earth, thou art beneficial in the necropolis. One makes for thee invocation-offerings; one celebrates for thee the *h3kr*-festival; one celebrates for thee the *w3g*-festival; one gives thee bread and beer from the altar of Khentamente; thou sailest down-stream in the *msktt*-bark; thou sailest upstream in the *mꜥndwt*-bark; one gives thee justification near every god. Be in thy own interest the most favourable one from among my dead, male and female! Thou knowest, he said to me: "I will report against thee and against thy children." Report thou against it! lo, thou art in the place of justification.[7]

It seems that for the people who wrote these letters, the boundary between this world and the netherworld could be crossed simply by writing a letter to the deceased.

---

[7] Piankoff and Clère (1934).

> A writing for Hetep-neb(i) and (?) Teti-sonbe. Have you really seen this remonstrance now that the two of you are there? Now if you would indeed be diligent on your (own) behalf, favour( ?) your children. May you then take hold of this dead man and/or this dead woman. May not the two of them(?) observe one fault of his, for there does not exist one who is vociferous against the two of you here.[8]

Form these letters, we witness a special character of the Egyptian mind, as people still alive would use written petitions to communicate with people in the netherworld. Although such letters did not survive in large numbers, they made an interesting contrast to the "appeal to the living" often found inscribed on the tomb walls. The letters were written by the living to the dead, while the appeal to the living was written by the dead to the living. Thus there was a two-way communication between the living and the dead.

It is clear that the funerary texts were geared toward making a safe passage for the deceased to reach the Land of Osiris or the Field of Offerings; thus, the expected result was the achievement of happiness, which is expressed succinctly in the *Book of the Dead* Spell 110:

> Beginning of the spells for the Field of Offerings, the spells for going forth by day, going in and out of the god's domain, attaining the Field of Rushes, existing in the Field of Offering, the great settlement, lady of the winds, gaining control there, becoming a blessed one there, plowing there, reaping (there), eating there, drinking there, copulating there, doing everything that is done upon earth.[9]

It is most revealing that this happy life, as it is expressed here, seems to be an ordinary life, doing everything that is done upon earth. If all the effort and all the struggle that the Egyptian had to pay and endure in order to reach the Land of Osiris were in the end an ordinary life on earth, it says something about the Egyptian mentality and about the values that the Egyptian held so dearly. The most precious life is also the most ordinary life.

In the non-funerary texts, there are also indications of how a happy and satisfactory life could and should be achieved. In *The Instruction of Hardjedef*, one of the texts that belonged to the genre of Wisdom Literature, the author gave the following advice to the young student:

> When you prosper, found your household,
> Take a hearty wife, a son will be born you.

---

[8] Simpson (1970).
[9] Allen (1974: 87).

> It is for the son you build a house,
> When you make a place for yourself.
> Make good your dwelling in the graveyard,
> Make worthy your station in the West.
> Given that death humbles us,
> Given that life exalts us,
> The house of death is for life.[10]

This simple wish—for the young man was to achieve a good or happy life by building a house, getting married, having a son, and founding a tomb for himself—echoes what was given in the *Book of the Dead* Spell 110 that an ordinary life is a happy life. Similar advice to the son is also found in the *Instruction of Any*, a text of the New Kingdom period:

> Take a wife while you're young,
> That she make a son for you;
> She should bear for you while you're youthful,
> It is proper to make people.
> Happy the man whose people are many,
> He is saluted on account of his progeny.[11]

> Learn about the way of a man
> Who undertakes to found his household.
> Make a garden, enclose a patch,
> In addition to your plowland;
> Set out trees within it,
> As shelter about your house.
> Fill your hand with all the flowers
> That your eye can see;
> One has need of all of them,
> It is good fortune not to lose them.[12]

Any also advised the son to build a tomb as early as possible, for one did not know when death will come and one better be ready for it:

> Do not go-out of your house,
> Without knowing your place of rest.
> Let your chosen place be known,
> Remember it and know it.

---

[10] Lichtheim (1975: 58).
[11] Lichtheim (1976: 136).
[12] Lichtheim (1976: 139).

Set it before you as the path to take,
If you are straight you find it.

Furnish your station in the valley,
The grave that shall conceal your corpse;
Set it before you as your concern,
A thing that matters in your eyes.
Emulate the great departed,
Who are at rest within their tombs.[13]

If we compare the instruction of *Any* and similar Wisdom texts about building a tomb with the Han Chinese authors' instruction of thrifty burial, the contrast is quite interesting. Thus far we have not found any advice from the Egyptian sages about a thrifty burial. It is probably unthinkable for the Egyptians, at least those who were in the position to give advice, to not want a well-equipped tomb for themselves and their descendants even though they advocated modesty and discouraged wanton desire. The Chinese authors who advocated thrifty burial, albeit never a majority among the intellectuals, had a long intellectual genealogy that was based on logical arguments about life and death and about the nonexistence of the soul or the netherworld.

At the end of the *Book of the Dead* Spell 125, it is declared that:

> He for whom this scroll is recited will prosper, and his children will prosper. He will be the friend of the king and his courtiers. He will receive bread, beer, and a big chunk of meat from the altar of the great god. He will not be held back at any gate of the west. He will be ushered in with the kings of Upper and Lower Egypt. He will be a follower of Osiris. Effective a million times.[14]

This is also another version of a happy life in the hereafter, doing whatever the deceased used to do on earth: eat, drink, and enjoy meat.

## Fear and Pessimism in Egyptian Texts

Yet despite the seemingly rational and modest approach to a happy life on earth as well as in the netherworld, there was also another equally real and common sentiment: the fear of death and the despair of losing a kinsfolk or a friend. This is abundantly expressed in the tomb paintings, represented by the group of

---

[13] Lichtheim (1976: 138).
[14] Lichtheim (1976: 132).

wailing women in the funeral procession. In the *Book of the Dead* Spell 175, we found a gloomy view of the netherworld:

| **Thus says N.:** | O Atum, how comes it that I travel to a desert which has no water and no air, and which is deep, dark and unsearchable? |
|---|---|
| **Atum:** | Live in it in content! |
| **N:** | But there is no love-making there! |
| **Atum:** | I have given spirit-being instead of water, air and love-making, contentment in place of bread and beer.[15] |

Here is a deep fear of the fate of the dead and death; even though the god gave assurance that the dead will be given "a lifetime of millions of years," the fact that the question was asked is an indication of the common sentiment of people when facing death.

In the tomb stela of Isenkhebe, a baby girl (or rather her parents) left a passage lamenting her premature death. The date of this stela has been assigned to the Saitic period (*c.* 650–630 BCE):

> I worship your ka, O Lord of Gods,
> Though I am but a child!
> Harm is what befell me,
> When I was but a child!
> A faultless one reports it.
> I lie in the vale, a young girl,
> I thirst with water beside me!
> I was driven from childhood too early!
> Turned away from my house as a youngster,
> Before I had my fill in it!
> The dark, a child's terror, engulfed me,
> While the breast was in my mouth!
> The demons of this hall bar everyone from me,
> I am too young to be alone!
> My heart enjoyed seeing many people,
> I was one who loved gaiety!
> O King of Gods, lord of eternity, to whom all people come!
> Give me bread, milk, incense, water that come from your altar,
> am a young girl without fault![16]

---

[15] Faulkner (1985, spell 175).
[16] Lichtheim (1980: 58–9).

The fact that the parents would make a tomb stela for their baby daughter says something about the special love of the parents toward the girl. Not many similar evidence had been preserved. Yet of course the sentiment expressed in the text was that of a mature person pondering upon the meaning of life and death, and a sense of despair when death comes.

In the tomb of Thothrekh, son of Petosiris, dated to the end of the Pharaonic period and the beginning of the Ptolemaic Dynasty, there is a passage that expressed similar sentiments:

> All who come to offer in this graveyard,
> Pronounce my name with abundant libation,
> Thoth will favor you for it.
> …
> Who hears my speech, his heart will grieve for it,
> For I am a small child snatched by force,
> Abridged in years as a little one,
> Like a man carried off by sleep.
> …
> I was rich in friends,
> All the men of my town,
> Not one of them could protect me!
> …
> Father and Mother implored Death;
> My brothers, they were head-on-knee,
> Since I reached this land of deprivation.
> When people were reckoned before the Lord of Gods,
> No fault of mine was found,
> I received bread in the hall of the Two Truths,
> Water from the sycamore as one of the perfect souls.[17]

A cup of fresh water was indeed the best gift in the desert. Yet although the land of eternity should be the paradise, the dead were not willing to give up what the world of the living could offer. Again this was the voice of the parents who expressed deep sorrow about the loss of their child, and while the entire text ends with blessings, the remorse and doubt about the intention of the gods could not really be contained. This, of course, should not be seen as only Egyptian, but rather a universal sentiment. As we shall see later, a Chinese tomb inscription of Eastern Han period of a child named Xu Aqu is strikingly similar.

---

[17] Lichtheim (1980: 53).

In a biographical inscription on a stela dedicated to Taimhotep, the wife of the high priest of Ptah at Memphis toward the end of the Ptolemaic period, we found a rather sober reflection about the frailty of life and resignation about the pervasive power of death. The theme of "follow your heart day and night" or *carpe diem* has already appeared in the Harper's Song discussed earlier. The inscription here makes another echo to the Harper over the distance of a thousand years:

> O my brother, my husband,
> Friend, high priest!
> Weary not of drink and food,
> Of drinking deep and loving!
> Celebrate the holiday,
> Follow your heart day and night,
> Let not care into your heart,
> Value the years spent on earth!
> The west, it is a land of sleep,
> Darkness weighs on the dwelling-place,
> Those who are there sleep in their mummy-forms.
> They wake not to see their brothers,
> They see not their fathers, their mothers,
> Their hearts forgot their wives, their children.
> The water of life which has food for all,
> It is thirst for me;
> It comes to him who is on earth,
> I thirst with water beside me!
> I do not know the place it is in,
> Since (I) came to this valley,
> Give me water that flows!
> Say to me: "You are not far from water!"
> Turn my face to the north wind at the edge of the water,
> Perhaps my heart will then be cooled in its grief!
> As for death, "Come!" is his name,
> All those that he calls to him
> Come to him immediately,
> Their hearts afraid through dread of him.
> Of gods or men no one beholds him,
> Yet great and small are in his hand,
> None restrains his finger from all his kin.
> He snatches the son from his mother

Before the old man who walks by his side;
Frightened they all plead before him,
He turns not his ear to them.
He comes not to him who prays for him,
He hears not him who praises him,
He is not seen that one might give him any gifts.
O you all who come to this graveyard,
Give me incense on the flame,
Water on every feast of the west![18]

The West described here seems different from the Land of Osiris or the Field of Offering that was given in the funerary texts. Here the world after death is a place of darkness, and the dead sleep in the mummy permanently and never would they awake to see their family again. Death is a terrifying tyrant that snatches away people with no mercy and no leniency. Such a gloomy view of the netherworld is rare in the long history of Egypt, and speculations have been made on the possible influence of foreign culture, as Egypt at the time had been ruled by the Greek Ptolemaic Dynasty for almost three hundred years.

This notwithstanding, no matter if the texts were optimistic or pessimistic, it seems that there was always a deep fear and insecurity behind the texts. When the text said that the dead will have a happy life in the netherworld, it could be a form of reassuring promise that was based on the fear that the dead might not be able to live a happy life after death. When the texts—the funerary texts such as the *Coffin Texts* and the *Book of the Dead*—laid out all sorts of dangers, challenges, or obstacles that the dead were supposed to encounter and were counting on the texts and the numerous deities for help, the fear of death was clearly expressed.

It has often been assumed that since the Egyptians believed in the idea of a blessed afterlife, their outlook to life must have been optimistic. Yet looking from the opposite side, there was also the possibility that, exactly because they held a basically pessimistic view of death and afterlife, the Egyptians needed to construct a paradise to offset their fear and uncertainty.

From the spells in the *Pyramid Texts* that tried to summon the deceased king to collect his bones and stand up, to the *Coffin Texts* in which the dead was reassured that he could assume his form and not be dismembered or petrified, to the *Book of the Dead* Spell 125 in which the deceased did his best to deny any

---

[18] Lichtheim (1980: 62–3).

wrongdoings lest he be condemned to a second death, we see a persistent and looming apprehension about death and the netherworld.

## Views of Happiness in Early Chinese Texts

Before venturing into the idea of happiness implied by the mortuary customs in early China, it is necessary to give a brief account of the views of happiness expressed in the early Chinese texts—shaped very much by the elite intellectuals—as a basis of discussion. According to the Confucian ideal, the most important task for a conscientious gentleman (*junzi* 君子) is to find a way to make the world a better place for the multitudes. Confucius emphasized personal cultivation as a precondition for a *junzi* to realize the ideals of benevolence (*ren* 仁), rightness (*yi* 義), propriety (*li* 禮), sagacity (*zhi* 智), and trustworthiness (*xin* 信). Mengzi (孟子 c. 372–289 BCE), one of the most important advocators of Confucian ideals, also talked about cultivation of the right vial energies (*qi* 氣). Yet his effort was mostly geared toward teaching the rulers ways to establish a benevolent government that could help the people to live a life free of want. Whether this could be considered a happy life or whether Confucius or Mengzi knew what the common people really wanted for a happy life could, of course, be subjects of further discussion.

Nonetheless, the concern with the cultivation of moral personhood in the lives of Ru (儒 educated officials) was the hallmark of Confucian teaching. Whether the cultivation of this moral personhood was also connected with the happiness of those who practice self-cultivation, as the Stoics might have insisted, however, did not seem to have been a central focus of discussion.[19] Presumably, the intended audience in such texts were the elites whose material need was not a concern. It can be said that, in the Confucian texts, moral rectitude and passion to serve in the government were the most important qualities of an educated person, so important that they might have eclipsed other human needs. In their discussions of good government, there was often the assumption that feeding the people well was a good enough achievement and that people would judge the ruler by whether he could supply a "good life," that is, material well-being,

---

[19] For a recent discussion, see Ivanhoe (2013). Ivanhoe argues that the Confucian idea of happiness is a kind of harmonious and satisfactory life among family, friends, and community on the one hand and ritual, culture, and tradition on the other. If we accept Ivanhoe's characterization of the Confucian idea of happiness, we could see that this is actually quite close to the ethical values found in Egyptian biographies and didactic texts.

to the people. This is expressed most famously by Mengzi's explanation of his ideal plan:

> For the people not to have any regrets over anything left undone, whether in the support of their parents when alive or in the mourning of them when dead is the first step along the Kingly way. If the mulberry is planted in every homestead of five *mu* of land, then those who are fifty can wear silk, if chickens, pigs and dogs do not miss their breeding season, then those who are seventy can eat meat; if each lot of a hundred *mu* is not deprived of labour during the busy season, then families with several mouths to feed will not go hungry. Exercise due care over the education provided by village schools, and reinforce this by teaching them the duties proper to sons and younger brothers, and those whose heads have turned hoary will not be carrying loads on the roads. When those who are seventy wear silk and eat meat and the masses are neither cold nor hungry, it is impossible for their princes not to be a true King.[20]

This was not an empty ideal invented by Mengzi to impress his audience, but a perennial concern of all governments in history, and could be a valid criterion for measuring a good government even today. However, there seems to be a "double standard"—in a good sense—here. While the elites considered material comfort a secondary concern in their lives—because they possessed a "higher" moral rectitude—they believed that the people (*min* 民) would be content and happy once provided with their material needs. This can be represented by the often-quoted passages from the *Analects*:

> The Master said, "Admirable indeed was the virtue of Hui! With a single bamboo dish of rice, a single gourd dish of drink, and living in his mean narrow lane, while others could not have endured the distress, he did not allow his joy to be affected by it. Admirable indeed was the virtue of Hui!"[21]
>
> The Master said, "With coarse rice to eat, with water to drink, and my bended arm for a pillow; I have still joy in the midst of these things. Riches and honours acquired by unrighteousness, are to me as a floating cloud."[22]

These words imply that life with coarse rice and plain water was not a comfortable one for average people, yet the Confucian intellectuals could take pleasure in it because they had a higher vision of life that could allow them to ignore

---

[20] *Mengzi zhushu* (1976; 1: 12.1–2); Lau (tr.) (2003: 7–9).
[21] *Lunyu zhushu* (1976, 6.9); trans. Legge (1960: 188).
[22] *Lunyu zhushu* (1976, 7.15); trans. Legge (1960: 200).

unpleasant material conditions.²³ By contrast, another passage from the *Analects* spells out the different needs of the common people:

> Zi Gong asked about government. The Master said, "The requisites of government are that there be sufficiency of food, sufficiency of military equipment, and the confidence of the people in their ruler." Zi Gong said, "If it cannot be helped, and one of these must be dispensed with, which of the three should be foregone first?" "The military equipment," said the Master. Zi Gong again asked, "If it cannot be helped, and one of the remaining two must be dispensed with, which of them should be foregone?" The Master answered, "Part with the food. From of old, death has been the lot of all men; but if the people have no faith in their rulers, there is no standing for the state."²⁴

This passage, however feudalistic to the modern eyes, basically says that for a government to stand, the trust of the people is most important. But the trust of the people is not easily established if material needs are not supplied, as Mengzi elaborated. If we put Mengzi's words, quoted previously, side by side with these words of Confucius, it seems that the Confucian thinkers were satisfied with providing a comfortable material life to the people, while they themselves considered self-cultivation as their duty and qualification as educators. Such self-cultivation, realized through the practice of observing benevolence, propriety, and compassion, has been a familiar topic of Chinese intellectual history. We can also find congenial spirit in the Egyptian wisdom texts when the sages advised their readers to exercise modesty and self-control and, acting as a benevolent mediator and educator, to serve the people in creating a harmonious society. Yet, unlike the Egyptian, the Confucian ethics did not leave much room to the will of gods to intervene with human affairs, as the importance of serving people took precedence over the service of gods and spirits. The *Analects* recorded a conversation between Confucius and a disciple named Jilu:

> Jilu asked about how to serve the ghosts and spirits. The Master said: "One could not yet serve humans; how could one serve the ghosts?" Ji Lu said, "May I ask about death?" The Master replied, "Not knowing [the meaning of] life, how could one know anything about death?"²⁵

This passage is often quoted as the epitome of the humanistic concern of Confucius, as he cared about this-worldly affairs while refraining from discussing

---

²³ Poo (2018b).
²⁴ *Lunyu zhushu* (1976, 12.7); trans. Legge (1960: 254).
²⁵ *Lunyu zhushu* (1976, 11.12); trans. Legge (1960: 240–1).

the unknown world of the dead or the spirits. Apparently only human affairs were relevant in the enterprise of building an ideal and presumably happy world.

Jilu's question about death, however, was answered by Zhuangzi (369–286 BCE) more than a hundred years later. Zhuangzi opened his essay on "Supreme Happiness" with the compelling questions:

> Is there such a thing as supreme happiness in the world or isn't there? Is there some way to keep yourself alive or isn't there? What to do, what to rely on, what to avoid, what to stick by, what to follow, what to leave alone, what to find happiness in, what to hate?[26]

These are sober reflections on the meaning of life even for modern readers. The tone of the questions reflects a chaotic time when people seemed to have lost a firm grasp of the meaning of life or the way to happiness. Zhuangzi then proposed a reply according to the commonly accepted idea of "desirable life" and "undesirable life" to establish a point of contention:

> This is what the world honours: wealth, eminence, long life, a good name. This is what the world finds happiness in: a life of ease, abundant food, fine clothes, beautiful sights, and sweet sounds. This is what it looks down on: poverty, meanness, early death, and a bad name. This is what it finds bitter: a life that knows no rest, a mouth that gets no rich food, no fine clothes for the body, no beautiful sights for the eye, and no sweet sounds for the ear. People who can't get these things fret a great deal and are afraid—this is a foolish way to treat the body.[27]

These two pictures of life—desirable and undesirable—may have a wider universal appeal beyond China, both then and now. However, as an unconventional and imaginative thinker, Zhuangzi quickly turned around—much in the spirit of Epicurus or Lucretius—and subverted these conventional views of happiness that the Confucians would be perfectly happy with. Zhuangzi employed a series of allegories to demonstrate his point:

> When Zhuangzi went to [Chu], he saw an old skull, all dry and parched. He poked it with this carriage whip and then asked, "Sir, were you greedy for life and forgetful of justice, and so came to this? Was your state overthrown and did you bow beneath the axe and so came to this? Did you do some evil deed or shameful wrong doings that brought disgrace upon your parents and family, and

---

[26] *Zhuangzi jishi* (1985: 608), trans. Watson (1964: 111).
[27] *Zhuangzi jishi* (1985: 609), trans. Watson (1964: 111).

so came to this? Was it through the pangs of cold and hunger that you came to this? Or was it because of your age that brought you to this?"

When he had finished speaking, he dragged the skull over and, using it for a pillow, lay down to sleep. In the middle of the night, the skull came to him in a dream and said, "You chatter like a rhetorician and all your words betray the entanglements of a living man. The dead know nothing of these! Would you like to hear an explication of death?" "Indeed," said Zhuangzi. The skull said, "In death there are no rulers above, no subjects below, and no chores of the four seasons. With nothing to do, our springs and autumns are as endless as heaven and earth. Even the happiness of a king facing south on his throne could not surpass this!"

Zhuangzi couldn't believe this and said, "If I got the Arbiter of Fate to give you a body again, make you some bones and flesh, return you to your parents and family and your old home and friends, would you want that?" The skull frowned severely, wrinkling up its brow. "How could I throw away the happiness of a king on throne and take on the toils of the human world again?"[28]

Zhuangzi's questions regarding how the skull came to its fate were intended to present a general view, not his own but that of the common people, of a good death or happy fate, since the skull is obviously not buried properly or ceremoniously, probably due to one of the reasons stated by Zhuangzi. The questions are of course posed only to allow the skull, in fact Zhuangzi himself, to present his view of death and happiness. That is, only in death can one find eternal peace, which may be regarded as the state of ultimate happiness. It is also a state free of all worldly concerns. This may be a dramatic and rhetorical presentation of his ideas, yet it is in tune with Zhuangzi's interest in advocating an unencumbered spirit that abhors the prevailing social conventions represented, at least partially, by the Confucian ideals. It also stands in drastic contrast to the ethos of Homer, when the ghost of Achilles says to Odysseus: "'Say not a word,' he answered, 'in death's favor; I would rather be a paid servant in a poor man's house and be above ground than king of kings among the dead'" (*Odyssey* 11, trans. Samuel Butler).

Zhunagzi was probably one of the earliest people in early China to give a positive evaluation of the world of the dead. It is interesting to note that this description of the world after death is directly related to the idea of searching for happiness. Zhunagzi's idea, of course, might have only been an idiosyncratic view regarding the nature of the world and the meaning of a happy life. By musing

---

[28] *Zhuangzi jishi* (1985: 617–19), trans. Watson (1964: 114–15).

on the absolute freedom and quietness of this world after death, the ideal happy life that Zhuangzi portrays was one that was quite opposite to the mundane life where the effort for a person to eke out a living was a constant pressure that only death could have brought to an end. This idea, though a little cynical or elitist, nonetheless carried some persuasion, as it was not without the support of realistic observations on the human conditions. Here the term used by Zhuangzi is *le*樂, which we translate as "joy" but could also signify "happiness."

There is no doubt that Zhuangzi took an extreme position in his contemporary world, no less as it is in the modern world. But this does not mean that his reflection was unique in history. We are reminded by the famous dictum of Solon, that a man is happy only when he is dead.[29] It seems that both had reached the same conclusion despite the circumstances that led to their realizations.

As a counterbalance to Zhuangzi's idea, the netherworld that we find in *Chuci*, though also from the South where Zhangzi originated, was rather the opposite of what Zhuangzi had imagined. A passage in *Chuci* has the following description of the netherworld when the soul was being recalled back to the world of the living:

> O soul, Go not down to the City of Darkness, where the Lord Earth lies, nine-coiled, with dreadful horns on his forehead, and a great humped back and bloody thumbs, pursuing men, swift-footed: Three eyes he has in his tiger's head, and his body is like a bull's.[30]

Instead of a peaceful and carefree environment, this world that the dead were destined to go was a horrifying place with threatening monsters and demons. One would therefore not want to go there for obvious reasons. People recall the soul of the departed, because this world was still better than the netherworld. For readers who might be familiar with contemporary Taiwanese folk customs, the ritual of recalling the soul, especially those who died in accidents, is still a living practice. It was an emotional reaction, though surely people would know this was a hope that was not going to be fulfilled. Now Zhuangzi's portrayal of a paradise-like netherworld might have been his own invention, the hell-like netherworld in the *Chuci* could probably have reflected some local beliefs in the Chu area where *Chuci* originated. Both, nevertheless, could be said to be based on certain assumptions about what is desirable in life, and what is not. If—as we shall not go into the Platonic discussion on the meaning of happiness—happiness

---

[29] *Herodotus* Book I: 86.
[30] Hawkes (1959: 105).

is having what one desires and fulfilling what one lacks, then clearly these ideas of the netherworld could be indicative of their contemporary sentiments about happiness, however partially or vaguely.[31]

Zhuangzi's writings might not have had significant impact on his contemporary public. But his stories about the skull and other characters did capture a glimpse of the chaotic social scene of the late Warring States period (476–221 BCE). What he attacked or ridiculed were, among other things, the prevailing social conventions of the time. Regarding funerals, for example, mortuary practices in Warring States and the Qin–Han periods (221 BCE to 220 CE) reflected a general belief that the dead should be supplied with abundant funerary objects to be used in the netherworld. The rationale motivating such mortuary practice was inevitably the assumption that what is lacking in life could be compensated for in death, and that if a person did not live a happy life on earth, he or she could have the chance to have an ideal life after death by having a proper burial. Mortuary practices reveal some clues as to how people in a society thought about happiness in life: to supply or not to supply the dead with particular types of objects and how much to supply are based on assumptions about the conditions or necessities for a happy life.

Such kind of care for the dead of an eager desire for a happy life, moreover, can be seen in a special category of funerary objects, the inscribed bronze mirrors that became prevalent during the Han period. The simpler inscriptions on the mirrors of the Han period often contain shorter sentences: "The family has lasting fortune and high prestig," "Happiness lasting forever," or "Great happiness, having what one wishes, for ever and ever, and having extended years and lifetime." Thus happiness consisted of the gaining of fortune, social prestige, and longevity.[32]

As the mirrors could theoretically be used by the deceased during their life time, we cannot exclude the possibility that, besides the practical use, they were meant to serve as auspicious objects in people's daily life. This is straightforwardly stated in an inscription:

> The first year of the Yungkang reign [167 CE] the wu-day of the first month, refining the tin and copper and producing the bright mirror. He who buys this will become extremely rich, and have prolonged life, such as that of the

---

[31] For a discussion of the meaning of "happiness" in early China from a philological approach, see Bauer (1976: 8–11). See also McMahon (2006: 1–15). McMahon argues that the Greek recognized that happiness was not what human beings could strive for, because the gods were unpredictable, and happiness, if understood in the original meaning of "hap," was basically what happens by luck.
[32] See in general Lin (1999).

King Father [of the East] and Queen Mother of the West. You shall attain high position, as far as the duke and marquis. You shall have longevity and great fortune, and long life as the Grand Master.[33]

Another inscription has the following sentences:

> This nice mirror is made in the year two of the Tianfeng reign [15 CE] It is hoped that you will enjoy lasting happiness and wealth and prestige in front of the sovereign, that you can always protect your parents and family, that when you serve in the government your position will be promoted to that of the high officials, and passing down the status to later generations forever.[34]

Yet the fact that they were found in tombs indicates that the happy life aspired in the inscriptions could equally serve as aspirations for the future of the deceased in the netherworld. Thus one mirror inscription says:

> The refined tin and copper is bright and clear, to use it to make mirror is suitable for decoration, it could prolong life and expel the inauspicious things. May you be like the sun light, lasting with the heaven for ever and ever with endless happiness.[35]

Here longevity, more than wealth and power, was appreciated. This is also echoed in another type of mirror inscriptions that aspire to life with the immortals:

> The shang-fang (official workshop) made this mirror and truly it is very fine. Upon it are immortal beings oblivious of old age. When they thirst they drink from the springs of jade; when they hunger they feed on jujubes. They roam at large throughout the world, wandering between the four oceans. They rove at will on the well-known hills plucking the Herb of Life. Long life be yours, like that of metal and stone, and serves as the protection of the country.[36]

The reference to the immortals may not be as contradictory to the idea of the netherworld as it seems, if we recall the Mawangdui silk paintings wherein figures of "heavenly officials" or auspicious signs such as the toad in the moon and the raven in the sun connecting to the myth of the Queen Mother of the West, who could dispense immortality, are all part of the picture. It also suggests that, to the people, the difference between the netherworld and the world of the immortals might not have been clearly defined. In this connection,

---

[33] Lin (1999: 283).
[34] Liu Yungming (1999: 4–5).
[35] Liu Yungming (1999: 4–5).
[36] Loewe (1979: 200–1).

it is worth mentioning that the main function of the tomb decorations was to provide a "program" of life—much as a set of funerary objects—that could be enjoyed by the deceased in a visualized form. Much in accordance with what we have gleaned from the mirror inscriptions, the tomb paintings and reliefs show scenes of daily life, mostly happy banquets, entertainments, carriage parades, official engagements, or auspicious omen signs such as the appearances of phoenix and immortals, even the Queen Mother of the West mentioned in the mirror inscriptions.[37]

However, it is also interesting to note that a certain sense of remorse, of regret, gained some position in the usually more optimistic mirror inscriptions. Thus we read sentences such as "As you departed in a haste, I am saddened. It will be a long time without seeing you, and it will be a rare occasion to serve you"[38] or "(Thinking that) we used to be together, I am saddened. The way is far, it will be a rare occasion to serve you."[39] It seems that such expressions are more suitable for a funerary setting, as the reference to the travel and the faraway destination hints at the way to the netherworld. Such sentiment is also reflected in an inscription found in an Eastern Han tomb:

> How hurting and sad, concerning Xu Aqu, who was just five years old, and yet left the bright world, to join the long night, without sun and stars. His soul dwells by itself, returned down to the darkness, separated forever from his family, with no hope of seeing his face.[40]

Just as those inscriptions that provide us with evidence of the aspiration for a happy life, the remorse about death and the grim prospects of the netherworld tell us from the reverse angle what people wished to have for a happy life. This, as we compare with the Egyptian evidence, says something universal in the human sentiments.

Other than the mirror inscriptions, the most direct textual testimony of the social and ethical values concerning the netherworld came from the so-called tomb quelling text (鎮墓文) or exorcistic text (解注文) and related material found in the tombs. As this textual genre has been extensively studied by Zhang Xunliao and Bai Bin,[41] we only need to point out that these texts were composed for the purpose of expelling bad luck and evil spirits—including the ghosts of

---

[37] For an overview, see Finsterbusch (1966–2000).
[38] Lin (1999: 165).
[39] Liu Tizhi (1979: 3157).
[40] Nanyang shi bowuguan (1974).
[41] Zhang Xunliao and Bai Bin (2006, vol. 1: 1–332).

the ancestors—for the living and helping the dead to lead a peaceful and happy life in the netherworld. We found this mentality prevailed throughout most of the tomb quelling texts. One example is a text quoted already in Chapter 4:

> Today is an auspicious day. It is for no other reason but the deceased Zhang Shujing, who unfortunately died prematurely, is scheduled to descend into the grave. The Yellow God, who created the Five Mountains, is in charge of the roster of the living, and recalling the *hun* and *po*, in charge of the list of the dead. The living may build a high tower; the dead returns and is buried deeply underneath. Eyebrows and beards having fallen, they drop and became dirt and dust. Now therefore I [the Messenger of Heavenly Emperor] present the medicine for eliminating poll-tax and corvée conscription, so that the descendants will not die. Nine pieces of ginseng [*renshen*人蔘] from Shangdang substitute for the living. A lead figurine [*qianren* 鉛人] is intended to substitute for the dead. The soybeans and melon-seeds are for the dead to pay for the taxation underground. The medicine of *lizhi* and *mouli* are to remove the earthly evil, so that no disaster will occur. When this decree arrives, restrict the officer of the Underworld, and do not disturb the Zhang family again. Doubly urgent as prescribed by the laws and ordinances.[42]

It is reveling in how far the bureaucratic mentality had penetrated into the imagination of the netherworld. What concerned people in the netherworld, from this bureaucratic perspective, was the need to pay taxes to the netherworld government. When the taxes are paid, as the text assured, the family members of the deceased should also be relieved of any misfortune. The last sentence of the text, "Doubly urgent as prescribed by the laws and ordinances," was a standard bureaucratic expression employed in government documents of the Han period and was employed by subsequent Daoist talismans indicating the source of authority. Another text, dated to 175 CE, has the following sentences:

> The Heavenly Emperor [issued] a decree, to secure the tomb of the local dead Xu Wentai. Command the Assistant of the Mount, the Lord of the Tomb, the Two-thousand-bushel of Underground, [who are] above, below, in the middle, to the left and right of the tomb, the Officer of the tomb gate, the Elders of Gaoli thus: Let the family and descendants of Xu Wentai not die again in the future. The heaven above is black, the earth below is misty. The dead returns to Yin, the living returns to Yang. The living has his district, the dead has his village. The living belongs to the [jurisdiction of] Changan to the West, the dead belongs to the [jurisdiction of] Mount Tai to the East. In happiness you should

---

[42] Zhang Xunliao and Bai Bin (2006, vol. 1: 160).

not miss each other, in distress you should not longing for each other. When the [god] of Mount Tai is to summon, use the gingsen to answer the call. If there should be punishment of culprit in the underground, the "honey figurine" should be substituting the dead. For thousands of years the living should never be inculpated. To help the living family members and descendants of Xu to become rich and powerful, with billions of wealth, and abundant descendants. Hereby I present gold and silver to satisfy the tomb owner, and seal the tomb ... The ancestors of the Xu family tombs and the grandparents [shall not] leave the tomb, and not to cause any damage, and each at peace in his place. When the tomb gate is sealed, the names pass on to later generations, and not causing [further] death. The rest is as what the Heavenly Emperor [used to] decree.[43]

For the user of the texts, therefore, there were two major concerns. On the one hand, the needs of the deceased in the netherworld, including daily sustenance, the handling of taxation, and corvée conscription, should be taken care of; on the other hand, the welfare of the living descendants should be protected by means of ritual pronouncements and magical objects such as ginseng. One persisting idea in these texts was that the dead should go his/her own way without any further engagement with the living. According to the interpretation of Zhang Xunliao and Bai Bin, these texts were the evidence of early Daoist ritual practice and belief. In this belief system, the ghosts of the deceased were potentially dangerous to the living, thus needed to be separated from the living by means of the exorcistic rituals, texts, and magical objects.[44]

It is worth noticing that not only the tomb quelling texts presented such kinds of mentality, but other funeral related texts also bear similar remarks. A text, dated to 79 CE, that served as passage document to the world after death has these words:

May living people not be encumbered with debt, may dead people not be penalized. The contract record is bright and clear.[45]

In another inscription found in a painted stone-brick tomb, the writer concluded that

He who is devoted to learning should rise to high position with office title; he who is to make a living out of commerce shall earn ten thousand times of profit

---

[43] Zhang Xunliao and Bai Bin 白彬 (2006, vol. 1: 163).
[44] Zhang Xunliao and Bai Bin (2006, vol. 1: 15–16).
[45] Harper (2004: 243).

daily. The deceased who descends to the dark region shall be separated [from the living], after the tomb gate is closed it will not be opened again.[46]

In a land-purchasing text (*maidi quan* 買地券) (dated 183 CE), a type of funerary text that imitated the legal land sale document, for the purpose of buying a piece of land from the netherworld government for the dead to use as burial site, it is advised thus:

> Ziqi (the deceased) shall eat the underground rice, follow the underground sacrifice; Ziqi shall eat the underground [food], follow the underground custom. The soul of the tomb owner (i.e. Ziqi) shall not blame Ziqi's wife, brothers, and parents. If he wish to blame [those who are alive], he should wait until the heads of the black bird become white, the horses grow horns, then he shall be heard [before the god].[47]

On the whole, therefore, one could confirm that based on the textual evidence, the imagination of the netherworld centered around the means to ensure a good life for the deceased. What seems more important, however, is that at the same time the welfare of the living was also taken care of, namely that the family members would become prosperous and have long and happy lives without the interference of the deceased. The purpose of the tomb quelling/exorcistic texts, in fact, was often pronounced at the outset as mainly for the benefit of the family members of the deceased:

> [On such and such day,] the Messenger of the Heavenly Emperor respectfully removes misfortunes and culprits from the Cao Bolu family, as far as thousand leagues … the living and the dead each go different ways, ten thousand leagues apart. From now on, the descendants are protected, and shall be long-lived like gold and stone, without any disaster. What is the guarantee? The divine medicine is the safeguard, and sealed with the seal of the Yellow God. In accordance with the law.[48]

Thus the texts reveal a potential tension between the living and the dead: as descendants and as filial sons and daughters, the living should theoretically show deep compassion for the deceased parents or family members; yet for practical protection, the belief in the potential trouble with the revenants required them to use the exorcistic/tomb quelling texts to keep the deceased at a distance. To put it in a more blunt fashion, it can even be said that, despite the prevailing social sanction of filial piety according to the Confucian persuasion, of respecting the ancestors, people who resorted to the use of the tomb quelling texts and the

---

[46] Ikeda On (1981: 214, no. 5).
[47] Zhang Xunliao and Bai Bin (2006: 206).
[48] Zhang Xunliao and Bai Bin (2006: 111).

kind of magical funerary objects actually showed a stronger tendency to acquire maximum benefit for the living by providing the funerary setup that will keep their ancestors at a distance. The hope that the descendants could become rich and famous and attain high government positions might have been unrealistic, yet it pointed at a popular mentality that manifested itself in the funerary settings.

## Comparative Note

The conceptualization of the netherworld and the measures that were prescribed to deal with the netherworld, therefore, seemed to have been conditioned by and evolved around the concern for the happiness of the deceased as well as the living. In both Egypt and China, people endeavored to supply the dead with a comfortable, if not a luxurious, life in the hereafter. Such behaviors must have originated from a primordial sentiment toward death and the afterlife. A happy life in the hereafter, revealed by the Chinese and the Egyptian evidence, is most likely similar to what people could have or hoped to have experienced in life. The rich burials in Egypt and China demonstrate clearly that "doing everything that is done upon earth"—as the *Book of the Dead* Spell 110 puts it—was also doing everything that is done upon earth according to one's status. The fear of death was inevitably intertwined with the hope to seek for a happy life; thus, the Egyptians used the funerary texts to ensure that the dead could attain a happy afterlife—according to what they thought best for a happy life on earth. The Chinese equally supplied the tomb with rich paraphernalia according to their status and ability. Both, however, were unable to eradicate doubts about the reality of the netherworld as a complete darkness. A Greek tomb epitaph sums up this doubt bitterly but also truthfully:

> Charidas, what is below?
> Great darkness.
> What about resurrection?
> A lie.
> And the God of the Dead?
> A myth. We perish utterly.[49]

The search for happiness was therefore an unending pursuit that vacillated between hope and fear and tumbled along the corridor of time.

---

[49] Sinclair (1967: 13–14).

# 7

# Conclusion

This comparison of ancient Egyptian and Chinese ideas of the netherworld is meant to create an opportunity to better understand both cultures through a specific lens. It is not primarily meant to revise our understanding of the details of their religious beliefs and practices, but to try to exercise the comparative method to understand how human societies constructed an ideal world or a paradise, to see what are the uniqueness or commonalities of these paradises, and to try to give an account of the rationale behind these constructions. As a socially constructed collective imagination, a paradise could be gained by posting it in the netherworld. Yet most likely some members of society would eventually consider that the idea of paradise is illusionary or difficult to confirm. This concluding chapter will therefore examine the ideas for and against the netherworld as a paradise and hopefully create a more nuanced understanding of both societies and their religious beliefs.

The key questions to be answered are set out in the introduction: Besides gaining some detailed understanding of each of the cultures, their visions of the netherworld, and the relationship between these visions and the quest for happiness, what new understanding of each society could be gained that would not be possible without the benefit of comparison? The example of ushabti and the "lead man" discussed in Chapter 5 demonstrates that comparison does yield new insights, as the presumably ordinary and noncontroversial sources could become unfamiliar and problematic once compared with other similar cases. The comparison should ideally lead to further questioning and eventually new understanding.

It is a useful exercise to reflect upon the discrepancy between the reality and the ideal. The conception of a netherworld and the search for happiness in ancient Egypt and China as we have seen in the sources represents the ideal or ideological construct, whereas the daily experience that comprises of all sorts of emotions—hopes and fears, joys and frustrations—was the social reality that formed the bases for the construction of that ideal. While thousands of years separate us from the ancient Egyptians and the ancient Chinese, we can nevertheless hope to approach their world because human beings as a species share a fundamental need for values and common aspirations for a happy life that is no less true today than thousands of years ago, which, as such, bridges the great divide. What we have seen in this study, therefore, are different ways to try to reach extra-human powers and the need to get rid of uncertainty about the future, and to fulfill the desire for happiness, which was perhaps never to be achieved, as revealed by traces of skepticism regarding the reality of the paradise.

It seems that even though both China and Egypt had a tradition of elaborate preparation for the afterlife, the relative importance of the conception of the afterlife in each tradition might not have been the same. In Egyptian religion, the idea of the afterlife occupied a key position in the belief system, especially for the ordinary people who aspired to become the residents of the Kingdom of Osiris. If this belief in the afterlife was to be extracted, then the entire structure of Egyptian religion would become disintegrated. This is because the existence of the afterlife upholds the operation of Egyptian social ethics, at least in theory. In ancient China, before the arrival of Buddhism and before Daoism became an organized religion, on the other hand, the idea of the afterlife circulating in society cannot be considered as having an intimate and vital relation with any "religious system"—since besides the government-sponsored state ceremony, it is difficult to identify any organized religious system and an operating clergy with a set of central tenets that hinged upon the idea of afterlife. At most it can be associated with certain disjointed beliefs, such as the belief in the "Controller of Fate" (*Siming*), the "Lord of the Underworld" (*Dixiazhu*), or the "Yellow God and the Big Dipper" (*Huangshen beidou*). We may say that the belief in the afterlife itself formed a subject of its own as an independent element in ancient Chinese religious beliefs, which was not connected with any "official cults," and had no direct relationship with the operation of social ethics and morality, until the coming of Buddhism. Compared with the idea of the afterlife in the ancient Egyptian religion, we can clearly see the different degrees of importance of this idea in the two societies.

Moreover, it seems that the more detailed and articulated the descriptions of the afterlife, the more important position the idea of the afterlife would occupy in the respective religious tradition. The nature of the deities, furthermore, was also a key factor in the formation of the idea of the afterlife. Whether divine justice exists, when will it be carried out, and in what form also affect the construction of the world after death. The idea of life—where does it come from and who controls it in each religious tradition—necessarily affects the imagination of the afterlife and the preparation for it.

What can be certain is that in both China and Egypt, the netherworld was imagined with reference to the world of the living, in particular the existence of a netherworld bureaucracy. However, how that netherworld bureaucracy was imagined differed according to their respective sociocultural and political situations. The Chinese bureaucracy of the Qin and Han Dynasties was way more complicated than the Egyptian bureaucracy, as witnessed the government structure from the central government down to the county- and village-level organizations.[1] The impact of this strong bureaucracy on the imagination of the netherworld, therefore, was deeper than that of the Egyptian netherworld, as we have seen far fewer details of worldly bureaucracy in the Egyptian religious texts. Instead, the Egyptian netherworld was filled with all sorts of deities, often in direct interactions or conversations with the deceased, which was rarely found in the Chinese netherworld, except in the literary texts of the late Han Dynasty and Six Dynasty periods.[2] The Han Dynasty funerary texts revealed much about how people perceived the function of the netherworld bureaucracy and what measures people should take to deal or negotiate with it.

On the other hand, the Egyptian funerary texts, represented by the *Pyramid Texts*, *Coffin Texts*, and *Book of the Dead*, are massive collection of magical spells that could help the deceased to conquer various challenges posed by netherworld deities and demons, so as to reach the land of Osiris. There was no actual dealing with the officials of the netherworld such as the tax assessors, but there was a constant fear that threatens the dead—fear of the numerous dangers and difficulties that the dead could encounter on the way to the paradise. The Han funerary texts, however, posed no such imagined challenge for the dead, as the fate of the dead was more or less clear in people's mind: the netherworld bureaucracy was predictable, like the one on earth.

One may have the impression that the Egyptian conception of the netherworld was basically a secured and optimistic one, at least for those who passed that judgment before Osiris. But deep down, there could have still been an uncertainty that loomed large in people's mind, because the funerary texts constantly reminded the dead about the possible danger in the netherworld; even if the person passes the judgment, and even though they were declared

---

[1] Bielenstein (1980); Loewe (2004); Poo (2018a, chapters 2 and 3).
[2] Poo (2022, chapter 4).

an innocent soul, his/her mind could still not be at ease, and need the help of the texts and spells. For the Chinese, death was generally recognized as the end of life, but with certain hope that the soul of the dead could still somehow continue to exist. The preparations for the funeral were hopeful gestures that people supplied to sooth the grief of the living, just in case the dead would need it. As for the fate of the dead, the Chinese of the pre-Buddhist era consigned to a netherworld that was very much the replica of this world, with very little elaboration of the threat of any netherworld monsters or deities. The python-like underground deity/monster that we saw in the late Warring State *Song of South* (*Chuci*) made no obvious impact on the Han imagination and was replaced by a group of underground bureaucrats. Literary expositions even confer upon this netherworld with all the vices and intrigues of the world of the living,[3] which never appeared in the Egyptian imagination. For although the Egyptian netherworld was full of all sorts of dangers and threats, they were never the kind of problems that a person was likely to have encountered in real life, such as dealing with corrupted underworld officials.[4] In other words, the Chinese imagination of the netherworld follows closely their life experience, while the Egyptian netherworld was one of fantasy that no living person could have experienced in real life.

If funerary setup could be seen as the outward expression of the idea of a happy life in the hereafter, the funerary texts could be seen as the inner principle. Egypt and China had similar outward expressions, as we laid out in Chapters 2 and 3, yet with quite different inner principles. As the texts reveal, the ethical principles that supported the funerary setup in China were this-worldly concerns, while those that supported the Egyptian funerary setup were aspirations for a just life while alive and a blessed afterlife when dead. The connection between ethical values and a happy afterlife was not at all strong in ancient China. This means that we should not give equal weight to similar phenomena, and hence we should reflect upon the meaning of the outward expression in each culture from a new angle. The happiness that the average ancient Chinese aspired to may outwardly be quite similar to that of the ancient Egyptian, yet the inside principles differed from each other.

At this point, an excursion of the nature of the Egyptian king and the Chinese emperor could perhaps demonstrate the difference of the two cultural systems.

---

[3] Poo (2022, chapter 4).
[4] Poo (2022, chapter 4).

## Conclusion

When Emperor Wen of Han (203–157 BCE) died, he left a will to state his position on death and burial rituals:

> I have heard that of all the countless beings beneath heaven which sprout or are brought to life, there is none which does not have its time of death, for death is a part of the abiding order of heaven and earth and the natural end of all creatures. How then can it be such a sorrowful thing? Yet in the world today, because all men rejoice in life and hate death, they exhaust their wealth in providing lavish burials for the departed, and endanger their health by prolonged mourning. I can in no way approve of such practices.
>
> I, who am without virtue, have had no means to bring succor to the people. Now that I have passed away, if I were to inflict upon them deep mourning and prolonged lamentation, disrupting the usual practice of the cold and hot seasons, grieving the fathers and sons of the people and blighting the desires of old and young, causing them to diminish their food and drink and to interrupt the sacrifices to the ancestors and spirits, it would only deepen my lack of virtue. What then could I say to the world?
>
> ...
>
> Let the official and people of the empire be instructed that, whenever this order shall reach them, they shall take part in lamentations for three days, after which all shall remove their mourning garments. There shall be no prohibitions against taking a wife or giving a daughter in marriage, or against performing sacrifices or partaking of wine and meat.
>
> ...
>
> After the coffin has been lowered into the grave, deep mourning shall be worn for fifteen days, light mourning for fourteen days, and thin garments for seven days, and then all mourning clothes shall be removed. Matters which are not specifically covered herein shall be conducted in accordance with the spirit of this order. All of this shall be announced to the people of the empire so that they may understand my will. The hills and rivers around my tomb at Paling may be left in their natural state and need not be altered in any way. The ladies of the palace, from those of the highest rank down to the junior maids, shall be sent back to their homes.[5]

Emperor Wen himself was known to be fond of the Daoist philosophy of following nature and allowing the people to recuperate after years of devastating wars that brought down the Qin Dynasty, by first reducing agricultural tax to one-thirtieth and then eliminated it entirely.[6] This lenient policy was passed

---

[5] *Shiji* (1962: 433–4), translation follows Watson (1968: 364).
[6] *Hanshu* 1135.

down to the next emperor, so that a period of prosperity of the country ensued, with the accumulation of great wealth for the central government.

Regarding death, Emperor Wen took a Daoist or naturalist way of looking at life and death as but the nature of all creatures. Thus there should be no reason for one to mourn death. Yet he recognized that people in society were accustomed to the habit of providing lavish burials for their deceased kin, which he did not approve of. While emphasizing that his subjects should not be over-disturbed or disrupted in their lives, he nevertheless allowed the people to observe some Confucian post-funeral mourning etiquettes.

To the Egyptian king, the kind of "confession" that Emperor Wen had expressed was of course impossible to think. This has to do with the ultimate statuses of the Egyptian king and the Chinese emperor. The Egyptian king was in effect the equivalent of God on earth, the guarantor of the entire human institution, and the only arbiter of every affair on earth. The king was in fact the state, and the state was what sustained the political ideology, the religious legitimacy, and the moral authority of the king. However, having great power and prestige, the king has no free will of his own in this system of political theology, but as a representative of the state, the Egyptian cosmos. The Chinese emperor, on the other hand, although also called "the Son of Heaven," comparable to the Egyptian king's title "Son of Ra," was in fact a student of history. His authority was derived from the mandate of heaven, which could be taken away if his behavior was not in accordance with the heavenly way. The mandate, moreover, had to be understood from a historical point of view. How a ruler in the past gained or lost his mandate could form important lessons for the present sovereign. His actions could still be fallible and subject to the scrutiny of the educated officials surrounding him. His personal character and inclination could produce grave consequences that may incur the wrath of heaven. This could not happen in Egypt by virtue of the king's sacred status.

The testimony of Emperor Wen shows an interesting blend of Daoist and Confucian ideas concerning death and funeral. In fact the division of "Daoist" and "Confucian" views is mostly our modern re-creation of the intellectual atmosphere in Emperor Wen's time. Assuming that the testimony was most likely composed with the help of his close advisors, the content could be seen as a representation of the contemporary elitist view of life and death, and the appropriate way of mourning. The text itself never mentions Laozi or Zhuangzi, but assumes that the naturalist view was the "natural" way of seeing things, certainly among the high elites of his time. The text also did not mention Confucius, but the mourning rules implicitly identified with what one could find in the Confucian texts such as the *Book of Ceremony* (*I-li*). Thus our modern habit of making sharp division between Daoist and Confucian conceptions at this time is most likely anachronistic.

Emperor Wen's "Daoist" view could be said as befitting the discourse of a group of Daoist-inclined intellectuals who made their idea of "thrifty burial" known from the late Warring States period and lasting into the Han.[7] Notable among these was Yang Wangsun, already mentioned in Chapter 5, who desired to be buried naked in an earth pit without any accompanying paraphernalia. Although a rather extreme position, his arguments were quite compelling in the context of an atheist and naturalist understanding of life and death:

> A lavish burial is of absolutely no benefit to the dead man, and yet foolish people strive to outdo each other in extravagance, wasting their money, exhausting their resources, putting it all into the ground to rot. In some cases they bury it today only to have it dug up tomorrow, so that the result is the same as if they had left the corpse lying out in the open fields.
>
> Now death is the transformation that comes at the end of life, the final return of all things ... Thus each thing returns to its true home in deep darkness, where there is neither form nor sound. Then it may achieve union with the essence of the Way. Outward decoration may dazzle the mob, but lavish burial erects a barrier to its goal, prevents that which is to be transformed from undergoing change ... I have heard that the spirit belongs to heaven and the bodily form belongs to Earth. After the spirit has left the form, then each returned to its true home. Therefore, the spirits of the dead are called *gui* (鬼), which is to say that they have "returned" (*gui* 歸). As for the body, it lies there all alone like a clod—how could it possibly have consciousness?[8]

Yang's idea stood out as one branch of Chinese intellectual tradition concerning the reality of life and death. Yet the reality is that even though many intellectuals of later generations agreed with his position in general, they had to yield to social customs of allowing a place for proper funerals.[9]

Finally, one may venture to summarize the nature of the ancient Chinese and Egyptian ideas of the netherworld based on the above comparison. The Chinese netherworld was modeled after the hierarchical world of the living, and no transcendental principles were applied, in the sense that the deceased were to

---

[7] Poo (1990).
[8] *Hanshu* 67: 2907–9, trans. Watson (1974:107–9).
[9] Poo (1990).

be transformed into a spiritual existence in paradise. There were no surprises and no threats from netherworld deities or monsters, but harassments from netherworld officials were expected. The "deities" in the netherworld, if they existed, seem to have assumed bureaucratic roles in the netherworld hierarchy. On the other hand, stories about ghosts appearing to the living were common, indicating that the line between the living and the dead was porous.[10]

For the Egyptian imagination, the various netherworld terrains that the deceased needed to pass through were similar to the worldly terrain that the living would have experienced. But the difficulties with deities and monsters that the dead were expected to meet in the netherworld were not likely the usual experience of the living. It is true, however, that the Egyptians had plenty of knowledge about the various images of the deities, depicted either on the temple walls or in the illustrations in the funerary texts such as the *Book of the Dead*. Thus it would not be completely out of their sphere of experience to imagine many deities in the netherworld. Information from literature can also support this observation: Stories such as the magicians at the court of King Cheops, the *Shipwrecked Sailor*, or the *Tale of the Two Brothers*, all involved supernatural phenomena and monsters or deities intervening in human affairs, thus making the threatening deities and monsters in the *Book of the Dead* not something completely out of people's imagination.

The Egyptian imagination of the netherworld could be understood as a narrative of fantasy stories that were constructed in the context of religious tenets: The dead, who were ideally justified and flawless souls, had to pass through all sorts of tests, with the help of magical spells and benevolent deities, so as to conquer all the difficulties and reach the final destination, the land of Osiris. It was a heroic story in search for happiness, cloaked in a religious framework.

This heroic story was no doubt based on the myth of Osiris, which was gradually formed during the Old Kingdom and further developed in the subsequent eras. By the New Kingdom it became one that was shared by "everyone" in society, for everyone would become an "Orisis NN" or an "Osirian," follower of Osiris, the hero-god who conquered death, was resurrected, and lived in the Western Paradise. This is a very different imagination compared with the Chinese one. The Chinese imagination was pragmatic, as life in the netherworld was imagined as "business as usual." The important concern was that the welfare of the dead and his family should be taken care of. There were no adventures waiting for the dead, and, before the coming of the Buddhist ideas of the Western Paradise

---

[10] Poo (2022b).

(or the Pure Land, *jingtu* 淨土), the Hell (*diyu*地獄, literally "underground prison"), and transmigration, the stay in the netherworld did not seem to have any prospect of ending. No text had mentioned anything about the future of the people in this world.

All the preparations for and imaginations about the netherworld that we have studied in this book were of course left by those who were alive while doing it. None of them, since they had long gone into that netherworld, could come back and tell us whether their view of the netherworld was true or not. The challenge for those of us who study attitudes toward death and afterlife is the same as the ancients: that probably none of us could describe what we would have thought or realized about all these questions, about the soul and the light in another realm, just moments before we pass on to the eternal darkness. The positive or optimistic view of the netherworld, expressed by the Egyptians as well as the Chinese, was a continuation of certain form of existence, each according to their socially conditioned imagination. For the Egyptians, it was a world where deities dominated and where the deceased played a cosmic role assigned by the belief system, without individual initiatives, as conforming to the rule of being a "blessed and faultless soul" had restricted all the individualities. For the Chinese, the netherworld was just as lively as this world, and people had to strive for success in life. That is, one still needed to actively search for happiness by doing what was required of a good citizen: paying taxes, submitting household registration to underground bureaucracy, bribing officials, and buying a piece of land to build a home. For them, there was no one-size-fits-all solution for achieving a happy life in the netherworld guaranteed by Osiris, as the Egyptians did.

There were, as we also noticed, negative or pessimistic views about the idea of a netherworld. The Harper's Song of the Egyptian Middle Kingdom tells of disillusion about a life after death, followed by the late period biographical texts that describe the land of the dead as a world of complete darkness. This distrust of the traditional religious tenet, the system of judgment after death, was an important reminder of the complexity of a living culture, wherein not everything was in sync and not everyone held identical values. On this point, the Chinese material shows greater variety concerning the idea of the world after death. While the mainstream majority might have conformed to a view of a netherworld dominated by underground bureaucracy, the alternative view of the nonexistence of the afterlife propagated by the Daoist-naturalist inclined elites was always visible in society, just as they played a significant role in real-world cultural landscape.

Death, according to the Daoist view, is a complete blackout in eternal time with no dream. The state of happiness in this dreamless land, as Solon or Zhuangzi described, would be just a little out of reach for those who are still alive. In any case, the idea of the netherworld did not limit the urge of the Chinese to seek for happiness, whether in this life or the next; the Egyptian idea of the netherworld, on the other hand, provided a land of happiness for everyone and therefore created a theoretically more secured afterlife, though not without the need to go through a process of self-cultivation in terms of moral rectitude.

It seems that for the Chinese, or the majority of them, the netherworld was a place where worldly affairs continued to take place. If the imagination of the netherworld could reflect the idea of a happy life, then the meaning of happiness was to be sought in a worldly context that had no mystery involved. For the Egyptians, if we take *Book of the Dead* chapter 110 as an ideal picture, the happy life in the Beautiful West was a hard-won one after a perilous journey, yet in the end it was also a replica of life on earth, doing whatever one used to do.

# References

Abt, Theodor, and Erik Hornung. (2003). *Knowledge for the Afterlife: The Egyptian Amduat—a Quest for Immortality*. Zurich: Living Human Heritage Publications.

Alexanian, Nicole. (2006). "Tomb and Social Status: The Textual Evidence." In *The Old Kingdom Art and Archaeology*, ed. Miroslav Bárta, 1–8. Prague: Czech Institute of Egyptology.

Allen, James P. (2005). *The Ancient Egyptian Pyramid Texts*. Atlanta: Society of Biblical Literature.

Allen, James P. (2006). "Some Aspects of the Non-Royal Afterlife in the Old Kingdom." In *The Old Kingdom Art and Archaeology*, ed. Miroslav Bárta, 9–18. Prague: Academy of Sciences of the Czech Republic.

Allen, Thomas G. (1974). *The Book of the Dead, or Going Forth by Day*. Chicago: University of Chicago Press.

Alster, Bendt, ed. (1980). *Death in Mesopotamia: Copenhagen Studies in Assyriology 8*. Copenhagen: Akademisk Forlag.

Arnold, Dieter. (1999). "Old Kingdom Statues in Their Architectural Setting." In *Egyptian Art in the Age of the Pyramids*, 40–9, figs. 19–21. New York: Metropolitan Museum of Art.

Assmann, Jan. (1995). *Egyptian Solar Religion in the New Kingdom*. London: Kegan Paul.

Assmann, Jan. (2002). *The Mind of Egypt: History and Meaning in the Time of the Pharaohs*. New York: Metropolitan Books.

Assmann, Jan. (2005). *Death and Salvation in Ancient Egypt*. Ithaca: Cornell University Press.

Baines, John. (1991). "Society, Morality, and Religious Practice." In *Religion in Ancient Egypt: Gods, Myths, and Personal Practice*, ed. Byron Shafer, 123–200. Ithaca: Cornell University Press.

Ban Gu 班固. (1962). *Hanshu* 漢書. Beijing: Zhonghua shuju.

Barbieri-Low, Anthony J. (2021). *Ancient Egypt and Early China: State, Society, and Culture*. Seattle: University of Washington Press.

Barbieri-Low, Anthony J., and Robin D. S. Yates. (2015). *Law, State, and Society in Early Imperial China: A Study with Critical Edition and Translation of the Legal Texts from Zhangjiashan Tomb No. 247*. Leiden: Brill.

Bard, Kathryn. (2012). *An Introduction to the Archaeology of Ancient Egypt*. Oxford: Blackwell.

Bárta, Miroslav. (1998). "Serdab and Statue Placement in the Private Tombs Down to the Fourth Dynasty." *Mitteilungen des Deutschen Archäologischen Instituts, Abteilung Kairo*, vol. 54: 65–75.

Bárta, Miroslav. (2005). "Architectural Innovations in the Development of the Non-Royal Tomb during the Reign of Nyuserra." In *Structure and Significance: Thoughts on Ancient Egyptian Archetecture*, ed. Peter Jánosi, 105–30. Vienna: Verlag der Österreichischen Akademie der Wissenschaften.

Bárta, Miroslav, ed. (2006). *The Old Kingdom Art and Archaeology*. Prague: Academy of Sciences of the Czech Republic.

Barta, Winfred. (1962). *Die Altägyptische Opferliste von der Frühzeit bis zur Griechisch-Römischen Epoche. Münchner Ägyptologische Studien 3*, Munich: Ugarit-Verlag.

Bauer, Wolfgang. (1976). *China and the Search for Happiness: Recurring Themes in Four Thousand Years of Chinese Cultural History*. New York: Seabury Press.

Belayche, Nicole. (2007). "Religious Actors In Daily Life: Practices and Related Beliefs." In *A Companion to Roman Religion*, ed. Jörg Rüpke, 275–91. Oxford: Blackwell.

Bielenstein, Hans. (1980). *The Bureaucracy of Han Times*. Cambridge: Cambridge University Press.

Bottéro, Jean. (1983). "Les morts et l'au-delà dans rituels en accadien contre l'action des 'revenants.'" *Zeitschrift für Assyriologie*, vol. 73: 153–203.

de Buck, Adriaan. (1935–61). *The Egyptian Coffin Texts*, 7 vols. Chicago: University of Chicago Press.

Chang, Kwang-chih. (1980). *Shang Civilization*. New Haven: Yale University Press.

Chavannes, Edouard. (1910) *Le T'ai Chan*. Paris: Leroux.

Chen Songchang 陳松長. (1998). "Zhanguo shidai bingsizhe de daoci 戰國時代兵死者的禱辭." *Jianbo yanjiu yicong* 簡帛研究譯叢, vol. 2: 30–42.

Chen Songchang 陳松長. (2001). *Xianggang zhongwen daxue wenwuguan cang jiandu* 香港中文大學文物館藏簡牘. Hong Kong: Chinese University.

Darnell, John C., and Colleen M. Darnell. (2018). *The Ancient Egyptian Netherworld Books*. Atlanta: Society of Biblical Literature.

Davies, Nina M. (1936). *Ancient Egyptian Paintings*. Chicago: University of Chicago Press.

Dreyer, Gunter. (1988). *Umm el Qaab I: Das prädynastische Königsgrab U-j und seine fruühen Schriftzeugnisse* (mit Beitragen von U. Hartung und F. Pumpenmeier und einem Anhang von F. Feindt und M. Fischer), *Archäologische Veröffentlichungen, Deutsches Archäologisches Institut Abteilung Kairo*, 86. Cairo: Deutsches Archäologisches Institut Abteilung Kairo.

Du, Shaohu 杜少虎. (2004). *Zhuobimiaocai: Luoyang Hanmuhua yanjiu* 拙筆妙彩：洛陽漢墓畫研究. Zhengzhou: Henan meishuchubanshe 河南美術出版社.

Duell, Prentice. (1938). *The Mastaba of Mereruka*, 2 vols, *OIP* 31 and 39. Chicago: University of Chicago Press.

Dunham, Dows, and William Kelly Simpson. (1974). *The Mastaba of Queen Mersyankh III (G 7530–7540). Giza Mastabas 1*. Boston: Museum of Fine Arts.

Eyre, Christopher J. (2009). "Belief and the Dead in Pharaonic Egypt." In *Rethinking Ghosts in World Religions*, ed. Poo, Mu-chou, 33–46. Leiden: Brill.
Fan Ye 范曄. (1965). *Houhanshu* 後漢書. Beijing: Zhonghua shuju.
Faulkner, Raymond O. (1969). *The Ancient Egyptian Pyramid Texts*. Oxford: Oxford University Press.
Faulkner, Raymond O. (1980). *The Ancient Egyptian Coffin Texts*. Warminster: Aris & Philippe.
Faulkner, Raymond O. (1985). *The Ancient Egyptian Book of the Dead*. New York: Macmillan.
Finsterbusch, Käte. (1966–2000). *Verzeichnis und Motivindex der Han-Darstellungen*, 4 vols. Wiesbaden: Otto Harrassowitz.
Forke, Alfred. (1962). *Lun Heng*, 2 vols. New York: Paragon Book Gallery.
Fracasso, Ricardo. (1988). "Holy Mother of Ancient China: A New Approach to the Hsi-wang-mu Problem." *T'oung Pao*, vol. 74: 1–46.
Gansusheng kaogu wenwu janjiuso 甘肅省考古文物研究所. (2009). *Tianshui fangmatan qinjian* 天水放馬灘秦簡. Beijing: Zhonghua shuju.
Gardiner, Alan H., and Kurt Sethe. (1928). *Egyptian Letters to the Dead, Mainly from the Old and Middle Kingdoms*. London: Egypt Exploration Society.
Garnot, J. Sainte Fare. (1938). *l'appel aux vivants dans les textes funéraires égyptiens des origins à la fin de l'ancien Empire*. Cairo: Institut français d'archéologie orientale.
Garstang, John. (1907). *The Burial Customs of Ancient Egypt*. London: Archibald Constable.
Goedicke, Hans. (1970). *The Report about the Dispute of a Man with His Ba: Papyrus Berlin 3024*. Baltimore: John Hopkins Press.
Grallert, Silke, and Wolfram Grajetzki, eds. (2007). *Life and Afterlife in Ancient Egypt during the Middle Kingdom and Second Intermediate Period*. London: Golden House Publications.
Griffith, J. G. (1960). *The Conflict of Horus and Seth*. Liverpool: Liverpool University Press.
Gu, Yanwu 顧炎武. (1970). *Rizhi lu* 日知錄. Taipei: Minglun Chubanshe.
Guo Qingfan 郭慶藩. (1985). *Zhuangzi jishi* 莊子集釋. Beijing: Zhonghua shuju.
Harper, Donald. (1985). "A Chinese Demonography of the Third Century B.C." *Harvard Journal of Asiatic Studies*, vol. 45: 459–98.
Harper, Donald. (1994). "Resurrection in Warring States Popular Religion." *Taoist Resources*, vol. 5, no. 2: 13–28.
Harper, Donald. (2004). "Contracts with the Spirit World in Han Common Religion: The Xuning Prayer and Sacrifice Documents of A.D. 79." *Cahiers d'Extrême-Asie*, vol. 14: 227–67.
Harpur, Y. (1987). *Decoration in Egyptian Tombs of the Old Kingdom: Studies in Orientation and Scene Content*. London: Kegan Paul International.

Hassan, Selim. (1960). *Excavations at Gîza*, vol. 9. Cairo: General Organisation for Government Printing Offices.
Hawkes, David. (1959). *Chu tzu: The Songs of the South, an Ancient Chinese Anthology*. Oxford: Clarendon Press.
Hayes, William C. (1946). "Egyptian Tomb Reliefs of the Old Kingdom." *The Metropolitan Museum of Art Bulletin*, New Series, vol. 4, no. 7 (March): 170–8.
Hays, Harold M. (2015). "The Entextualization of the Pyramid Texts and the Religious History of the Old Kingdom." In *Towards a New History for the Egyptian Old Kingdom: Perspectives on the Pyramid Age*, ed. P. D. Manuelian and T. Schneider, 199–226. Leiden: Brill.
Hebei Research Institute of Cultural Relics. (1990). *Anping Donghan bihuamu*安平東漢壁畫墓. Beijing: Wenwu.
Herodotus. (1975). *Histories*. Trans. A. D. Godley. Cambridge: Harvard University Press.
Hoffman, Michael A. (1979). *Egypt before the Pharaohs*. New York: Dorset.
Hornung, Erik. (1982). *Conception of God in Ancient Egypt: The One and the Many*. Ithaca: Cornell University Press.
Hornung, Erik. (1992). "Zur Struktur des ägyptischen Jenseitsglaubens." *ZÄS*, vol. 119: 124–30.
Hornung, Erik. (1999). *The Ancient Egyptian Books of the Afterlife*. Ithaca: Cornell University Press.
*Huainanzi* 淮南子. (1971). Taipei: Zonghua shuju.
Huan, Kuan 桓寬. (1992). *Yantielun* 鹽鐵論. Beijing: Zhonghua shuju.
Huang, Pei-xan 黃佩賢. (2008). *Handai mushi bihua yanjiu* 漢代墓室壁畫研究. Beijing: Wenwu.
Huang, Tzu-Hsuan. (2015). *Cataloguing Images for Life Six Feet Under: A Comparative Study on Old Kingdom Egyptian and Han Chinese*. Ph.D. dissertation. Hong Kong: Chinese University of Hong Kong.
Huang, Zhanyue黃展岳. (1990). *Zhongguo gudai de rensheng renxun* 中國古代的人牲人殉. Beijing: Wenwu.
Huang, Xiaofen黃曉芬. (2003). *Hanmu de kaoguxue yanjiu*漢墓的考古學研究, Hunan: Yuelushushe.
Huang, Yafeng黃雅峰 and Chen, Changshan陳長山 eds. (2008). Nanyang qilingang han huaxiangshimu南陽麒麟崗漢畫像石墓. Xian: Sanqin chubanshe.
Hubeisheng bowuguan 湖北省博物館. (1989). *Zenghou Yi mu* 曾侯乙墓, 2 vols. Beijing: Wenwu chubanshe.
Hubeisheng wenwu kaogu yanjiu suo湖北省文物考古研究所. (1995). *Jiangling Jiudian Dong Zhou mu*江陵九店東周墓. Beijing: Kexue chubanshe.
Hubeisheng wenwu kaogu yanjiusuo 湖北省文物考古研究所and Beijing daxue zhongwenxi北京大學中文系. (2000). *Jiudian Chujian*九店楚簡. Beijing: Zhonghua shuju.

Hunansheng bowuguan湖南省博物館 and Zhongguo kexueyuan kaogu yanjiusuo中國科學院考古研究所. (1973). *Changsha Mawangdui yihao Hanmu* 長沙馬王堆一號漢墓, 2 vols. Beijing: Wenwu chubanshe.

Hunansheng bowuguan湖南省博物館 and Hunan sheng wenwu gaogu yanjiusuo湖南省文物考古研究所. (2004). *Changsha Mawangdui er san hao Hanmu* 長沙馬王堆二、三號漢墓, vol. 1. Peking: Wenwu.

Ikeda On池田溫. (1981). "Chûgoku rekidai boken riakukô中國歷代墓券略考." *Tôyôbunka kenkyûjo kiyô*東洋文化研究所紀要, vol. 86: 193–278.

Ivanhoe, Philip J. (2013). "Happiness in Early Chinese Thought." In *Oxford Handbook of Happiness*, eds. Ilona Boniwell and Susan David. Oxford: Oxford University Press.

Jacq, C. (1986). *Le Voyage dans l'autre monde selon l'Égypte ancienne: épreuves etmétamorphoses du mort d'après les textes des pyramides et les textes des sarcophagus.* Monaco: La Rocher.

James, Jean M. (1995). "An Iconographic Study Xiwangmu during the Han dynasty." *Artibus Asiae*, vol. 55: 17–41.

Jánosi, Peter. (2002). "Aspects of Mastaba Development: The Position of Shafts and the Identification of Tomb Owners." In *Abusir and Saqqara in the year 2001. Archiv Orientální* 70, No. 3, ed. Filip Coppens, 337–50. Prague: Oriental Institute, Academy of Sciences of the Czech Republic.

Jiang Shoucheng 姜守誠. (2013). "Fangmatan Qinjian zhiguai gushi zhongde zongjiao xinyang放馬灘秦简《志怪故事》中的宗教信仰." *Shijie zongjiao yanjiu* 世界宗教研究, no. 5: 160–75.

Jiang Shoucheng 姜守誠. (2014). "Beida Qinjian Taiyuan you sizhe kaoshi 北大秦簡泰原有死者考釋." *Zhonghua wenshi luncong* 中華文史論叢 vol. 3: 143–78.

Jiangsusheng wenwu guanli weiyuanhui江蘇文物管理委員會. (1960). "Jiangsu gaoyiu shaojiagou handai yizhi de qingli江蘇高郵邵家溝漢代遺址的清理." *Kaogu*考古, vol. 10: 18–23.

Jin, Weino 金維諾, and Nie, Chongzheng聶崇正, eds. (2009). *Zhongguo meishu quanji, juanzhouhua,*中國美術全集·卷軸畫, vol. 1. Hefei: Huangshan chuban she.

Jinancheng Fenghuangshan 168 hao Hanmu fajue zhenglizu 紀南城鳳凰山一六八號漢墓發掘整理組. (1975). "Hubei Jiangling Fenghuangshan168 hao Hanmu fajue jianbao湖北江陵鳳凰山一六八號漢墓發掘簡報." *Wenwu*, vol. 9: 1–7.

Jones, H. M. (1953). *The Pursuit of Happiness*. Ithaca: Cornell University Press.

Junker, Hermann. (1955). *Gîza 12. Schlußband mit Zusammenfassungen und Gesamt-Verzeichnissen von Band 1–12.* Akademie der Wissenschaften in Wien Philosophisch-historische Klasse Denkschriften 75, Abhandlung 2. Vienna: Rudolph M. Rohrer.

Kanawati, Naguib. (2001). *The Tomb and Beyond: Burial Customs of Egyptian Officials.* Warminster: Aris & Phillips.

Kawanati, Naguib. (2010). *Decorated Burial Chambers of the Old Kingdom.* Cairo: Supreme Council of Antiquities.

Kees, H. ([1926] 1983). *Totenglauben und Jenseitsvorstellungen der alten Aegypter.* Leipzig: J. C. Hinrichs.

Kemp, B. J. (1995). "How Religious were the Ancient Egyptians?" *Cambridge Archaeological Journal*, vol. 5, no. 1: 25–54.

Lacau, Pierre. (1910). *Textes religieux égyptiens.* Paris: Librairie Honoré Champion.

Lagerwey, John, and Marc Kalinowski, eds. (2009). *Early Chinese Religion, Part One: Shang through Han (1250 BC–220 AD).* Leiden: Brill.

Lai, Guolong. (2015). *Excavating the Afterlife: The Archaeology of Early Chinese Religion.* Seattle: University of Washington Press.

Lau, D. C. (2003). *Mencius. A Bilingual Edition.* Hong Kong: Chinese University Press.

Leclant, J. (1975). "Earu-Gefilde." In *Lexikon der Ägyptologie*, Vol. 1, 1156–60. Wiesbaden: Otto Harrassowitz.

Legge, James. (1960). *The Chinese Classics*, 5 vols. Hong Kong: Hong Kong University Press.

Lehner, Mark. (1997). *The Complete Pyramid.* London: Thames and Hudson.

Lesko, L. H. (1971–2). "The Field of Hetep in Egyptian Coffin Texts." *Journal of the American Research Center in Egypt*, vol. 9: 89–101.

Li, Ling 李零. (2012). "Beida Qinjian Taiyuan you sizhe jianjie 北大秦簡泰原有死者簡介." *Wenwu*, vol. 6: 81–4.

Li, Falin 李發林 (1982). *Shangdong Hanhuaxiangshi Yanjiu* 山東漢畫像石研究. Yinan: Qilushushe 齊魯書社.

Li, Xiaoxuan 李小旋. (2016). "Cong mawangdui dao jinqueshan: xihan guangai bohua bijiao yenjiu 從馬王堆到金雀山——西漢棺蓋帛畫比較研究." *Yishu tansuo* 藝術探索, vol. 3: 92–8.

Li, Xueqin 李學勤 (1990). "Fangmatan jien zhong de zhiguai gushi 放馬灘簡中的志怪故事." *Wenwu*, vol. 4: 43–4.

Lichtheim, Miriam. (1975). *Ancient Egyptian Literature vol. I.* Berkeley: University of California Press.

Lichtheim, Miriam. (1976). *Ancient Egyptian Literature vol. II.* Berkeley: University of California Press.

Lichtheim, Miriam. (1980). *Ancient Egyptian Literature vol. III.* Berkeley: University of California Press.

Lichtheim, Miriam. (1992). *Maat in Egyptian Autobiographies and Related Studies.* (Orbis Biblicus et Orientalis). Fribourg: University Press.

Lichtheim, Miriam. (1997). *Moral Values in Ancient Egypt* (Orbis Biblicus et Orientalis 155). Fribourg: University Press.

De Ligt, Luuk. (2003). "Taxes, Trade, and the Circulation of Coin: The Roman Empire, Mughal India and T'ang China Compared." *Medieval History Journal*, vol. 6, no. 2: 231–48.

Liang, Siyong 梁思永, and Gao, Quxun 高去尋. (1963). *Houjiazhuang di er ben 1001 hao damu* 侯家莊第二本 1001號大墓. Taipei: Academia Sinica.

*Liji zhengyi* 禮記正義. (1976). In *Shisanjing zhushu* 十三經注疏. By Ruan Yuan 阮元. Taipei: Yiwen chubanshe.

Lin Suqing 林素清. (1999). "Liang-Han jingming huibian 兩漢鏡銘彙編." In *Gu wenzixue lunwenji* 古文字學論文集, eds. Zhou Fengwu 周鳳五 and Lin Suqing 林素清, 235–312. Taipei: Guoli bianyiguan.

Linyi Jinqueshan Hanmu fajuezu 臨沂金雀山漢墓發掘組. (1977). "Shandong Linyi Jinqueshan jiuhao Hanmu fajue jianbao 山東臨沂金雀山九號漢墓發掘簡報." *Wenwu* 文物, vol. 11: 24–7.

Liu Tizhi 劉體智. (1979). *Xiao jiaojingge jinshi wenzi* 小校經閣金石文字 (五). Taipei: Taiwan datong shuju.

Liu Tseng-gui 劉增貴. (1997). "Handai de Taishan xinyang 漢代的泰山信仰." *Dalu zazhi* 大陸雜誌, vol. 94, no. 5: 193–205.

Liu Yungming 劉永明. (1999). *Han Tang jinianjing tulu* 漢唐紀年鏡圖錄. Beijing: Fenghuang chubanshe.

Liu Zhiyuan 劉志遠. (1958). *Sichuan handai huaxiangzhuan yishu* 四川漢代畫像磚藝術. Beijing: Zhongguo gudian yishu chubanshe.

Lloyd, G. E. R. (1996). *Adversaries and Authorities: Investigations into Ancient Greek and Chinese Science*. Cambridge: Cambridge University Press.

Lloyd, G. E. R. (2002). *The Ambitions of Curiosity: Understanding the World in Ancient Greece and China*. Cambridge: Cambridge University Press.

Lloyd, G. E. R. (2006). *Principles and Practices in Ancient Greek and Chinese Science*. Aldershot: Ashgate.

Lloyd, Geoffrey E. R., and Jingyi J. Zhao, eds. (2018). *Ancient Greece and China Compared*. Cambridge: Cambridge University Press.

Loewe, Michael. (1979). *Ways to Paradise: The Chinese Quest for Immortality*. London: George Allen and Unwin.

Loewe, Michael. (1985). "Interpreting Han Funerary Art: The Importance of Context." *Oriental Arts*, vol. 31, no. 3: 283–92.

Loewe, Michael. (2004). *The Men Who Governed China in Han Times*. Leiden: Brill.

Loyangshi dier wenwu gongzuodui 洛陽市第二文物工作隊, Huang Minglan 黃明蘭, and Guo Yinqiang 郭引強, eds. (1996). *Loyang Hanmu bihua* 洛陽漢墓壁畫. Beijing: Wenwu chubanshe.

Lu Xun 魯迅. (1986). *Guxiaoshuo gouchen* 古小說鉤沈. Taipei: Tangshan reprint.

Luiselli, Maria Michela. (2013). "Images of Personal Religion in Ancient Egypt: An Outline." In *Kult und Bild, Die bildliche Dimension des Kultes im Alten Orient, in der Antike und in der Neuzeit*, eds. Maria Michela Luiselli, Jürgen Mohn, and Stephanie Gripentrog, 13–40. Würzburg: Ergon Verlag.

*Lunyu zhushu* 論語注疏. (1976). In *Shisanjing zhushu* 十三經注疏. By Ruan Yuan 阮元. Taipei: Yiwen chubanshe.

Maspero, Gaston. (1893). *Les inscriptions des Pyramides de Saqqarah*. Paris: E. Bouillon.

McMahon, Daren. M. (2006). *Happiness, a History*. New York: Atlantic Monthly Press.

*Mengzi zhushu*孟子注疏. (1976). In *Shisanjing zhushu*十三經注疏. By Ruan Yuan阮元. Taipei: Yiwen chubanshe.

Meskell, Lynn. (1999). "Archaeologies of Life and Death." *American Journal of Archaeology*, vol. 103, no. 2: 181–99.

Morales, Antonio J. (2015). "Iteration, Innovation und Dekorum in Opferlisten des Alten Reichs. Zur Vorgeschichte der Pyramidentexte." *Zeitschrift für Ägyptische Sprache und Altertumskunde*, vol. 142, no. 1: 55–69.

Morenz, Siegfried. (1973). *Egyptian Religion*. Ithaca: Cornell University Press.

Mutschler, Fritz-Heiner, and Achim Mittag, eds. (2008). *Conceiving the Empire: China and Rome Compared*. Oxford: Oxford University Press.

Nanyang shi bowuguan 南陽市博物館. (1974). "Nanyang faxian Dong Han Xu Aqu muzhi huaxiangshi南陽發現東漢許阿瞿墓志畫象石." *Wenwu* 文物, vol. 8: 73–5.

Naville, E. (1886). *Das ägyptische Todtenbuch der XVIII. Bis XX Dynastie*. Berlin: A. Asher.

Nei Menggu zizhiqu boweguan wenwu gongzuodui 內蒙古自治區博物館文物工作隊. (1978). *Helin geer Hanmu bihua* 和林格爾漢墓壁畫. Peking: Wenwu.

Newberry, Percy E. (1890–2). *Beni Hasan*, vols. I and II. London: Egypt Exploration Fund.

Nylan, Michael. (2001). *The Five "Confucian" Classics*. New Haven: Yale University Press.

O'Connor, David. (2011). *Abydos, Egypt's First Pharaohs and the Cult of Osiris*. London: Thames and Hudson.

Petrie, Flinders, and James Quibell. (1896). *Naqada and Ballas*. London: B. Quaritch.

Piankoff, Alexander, and J. J. Clère. (1934). "A Letter to the Dead on a Bowl in the Louvre." *Journal of Egyptian Archaeology*, vol. 20, no. 3/4: 157–69.

Pirazzoli-T'Serstevens, Michèle. (2009). "Death and the Dead: Practices and Images in the Qin and Han." In *Early Chinese Religion Part I: Shang through Han (1250 BC–220 AD)*, eds. John Lagerwey and Marc Kalinowski, 949–1026. Leiden: Brill.

Poo, Mu-chou (Pu Muzho) 蒲慕州. (1987). "Wugu zhihuo de zhengzhi yiyi巫蠱之禍的政治意義," *Lishi yuyan yanjiuso jikan* 歷史語言研究所集刊, vol. 57, no. 3: 511–38.

Poo, Mu-chou. (1990). "Ideas Concerning Death and Burial in Pre-Han and Han China." *Asia Major* (3rd series), vol. 3, no. 2: 25–62.

Poo, Mu-chou (Pu Mu-zhou) 蒲慕州. (1993). *Muzang yu shensi* 墓葬與生死. Taipei: Lianjing.

Poo, Mu-chou. (1994). "The Emergence of Cultural Consciousness in Ancient Egypt and China: A Comparative Perspective." In *Essays in Egyptology in Honor of Hans Goedicke*, eds. Betsy M. Bryan and David Lorton, 191–200. San Antonio: Van Siclen Books.

Poo, Mu-chou. (1995). "The Images of Immortals and Eminent Monks: Religious Mentality in Early Medieval China." *Numen*, vol. 42: 172–96.

Poo, Mu-chou. (1997). "The Completion of an Ideal World: The Human Ghost in Early Medieval China." *Asia Major*, vol. 10: 69–94.

Poo, Mu-chou. (1998). *In Search of Personal Welfare.* Albany: State University of New York Press.

Poo, Mu-chou. (2000). "Ghost Literature: Exorcistic Ritual Texts or Daily Entertainment?" *Asia Major* 3rd series, vol. 13, no. 1: 43–64.

Poo, Mu-chou. (2003). "Egyptology and Comparative Ancient History," *Proceedings of the Eighth International Congress of Egyptologists*, vol. 2, 448–454. Cairo: American University in Cairo Press.

Poo, Mu-chou. (2004). "The Concept of Ghost in Ancient Chinese Religion." In *Chinese Religion and Society*, vol. 1, ed. John Lagerwey, 173–91. Hong Kong: Chinese University Press.

Poo, Mu-chou. (2005). *Enemies of Civilization: Attitudes toward Foreigners in Ancient Mesopotamia, Egypt, and China.* Albany: State University of New York Press.

Poo, Mu-chou, ed. (2009). *Rethinking Ghosts in World Religions.* Leiden: Brill.

Poo, Mu-chou. (2011a). "Preparation for the Afterlife in Ancient China." In *Mortality in Traditional Chinese Thought*, eds. Philip J. Ivanhoe and Amy Olberding, 13–36. Albany: State University of New York Press.

Poo, Mu-chou. (2011b). "Wisdom Literature in Comparison: Ancient Egypt and China." In *Achievements and Problems in Modern Egyptology*, eds. Galina A. Belova and Sergej V. Ivanov, 297–311. Moscow: Russian Academy of Science.

Poo, Mu-chou. (2018a). *Daily Life in Ancient China.* Cambridge: Cambridge University Press.

Poo, Mu-chou. (2018b). "Death and Happiness: Han China." In *Cultivating a Good Life in Early Chinese and Ancient Greek Philosophy: Perspectives and Reverberations*, eds. Kayrn Lai, Rick Benitez, and Hyun Jin Kim, 237–51. London: Bloomsbury.

Poo, Mu-chou. (2022a). "The Axial Age in Light of the Earliest Burial Customs of Ancient Egypt." In *The Star Who Appears in Thebes: Studies in Honour of Jiro Kondo*, eds. Nozomu Kawai and Benedict G. Davies, 339–50. Wallasey: Abercromby Press.

Poo, Mu-chou. (2022b). *Ghosts and Religious Life in Early China.* Cambridge: Cambridge University Press.

Poo, Mu-chou (Pu Muzhou). (2023). *Han Tang de wugu yu jiti xintai* 漢唐的巫蠱與集體心態. Taipei: Lianjing.

Poo, Mu-chou, Harold Drake, and Lisa Raphals, eds. (2017). *Old Society, New Belief: Religious Transformation of China and Rome, ca. 1st–6th Centuries.* Oxford: Oxford University Press.

Porter, B., and R. L. B. Moss. (1960). *Topographical Bibliography of Ancient Egyptian Hieroglyphic Texts, Reliefs, and Paintings*, vol. 1, The Theban Necropolis Part 1. Private Tombs. Oxford: Griffith Institute.

Qiu, Yongsheng 邱永生, Wei Ming 魏鳴, Li Xiaohui 李曉暉, and Li Yinde 李銀德. (1988). "Xuzhou beidongshan xihanmu fajue jianbao 徐州北洞山西漢墓發掘簡報." *Wenwu*, vol. 2: 2–18, 68.

Raphals, Lisa A. (1992). *Knowing Words: Wisdom and Cunning in the Classical Traditions of China and Greece.* Ithaca, NY: Cornell University Press.

Raphals, Lisa A. (2013). *Divination and Prediction in Early China and Ancient Greece*. Cambridge: Cambridge University Press.

Reisner, G. A. (1942). *A History of the Giza Necropolis*. Cambridge, MA: Harvard University Press.

Richards, Janet. (2005). *Society and Death in Ancient Egypt: Mortuary Landscapes of the Middle Kingdom*. New York: Cambridge University Press.

Ruan Yuan 阮元. (1976). *Lunyu zhushu* 論語注疏. *Shisanjing zhushu* 十三經注疏. Taipei: Yiwen chubanshe.

Ruan Yuan 阮元. (1976). *Zuozhuan zhengyi* 左傳正義. *Shisanjingzhushu* 十三經注疏. Taipei: Yiwen chubanshe.

Saleh, M., and H. Sourouzian. (1986). *Offiziller Katalog Die Hauptwerke im Aegyptischen Museum Kairo*. Mainz: Philipp von Zabern.

Scheidel, Walter, ed. (2009). *Rome and China: Comparative Perspectives on Ancient World Empires*. Oxford Oxford University Press.

Scheidel, Walter, ed. (2015). *State Power in Ancient China and Rome*. Oxford: Oxford University Press.

Seidel, Anna. (1987). "Traces of Han Religion in Funeral Texts Found in Tombs." In *Dokyō to shukyō bunka*, ed. Akitsuki Kan'ei, 21–57. Tokyo: Hirakawa.

Sethe, Kurt. (1908–22). *Die altägyptische Pyramidentexts*. Leipzig: J. C. Hinrichs.

Sethe, Kurt. (1932–3). *Urkunden des agyptischen Altertums*. Vol. I, *Urkunden des alten Reiches*. 2nd ed. Leipzig.

Shaanxi sheng kaogu yanjiusuo 陝西省考古研究所 and Xian Jiaotong daxue 西安交通大學 (1991). *Xian Jiaotong daxue XiHan bihuamu* 西安交通大學西漢壁畫墓. Xian: Jiaotong Daxue.

Shangdong Province Museum山東省博物館 and Shangdong Province Institute of Antiquity and Archaeology山東省文物考古研究所. (1982). *Shangdong Hanhuaxiangshi Xuanji*山東漢畫像石選集. Yinan: Qilushushe齊魯書社.

Shankman, Stephen, and Stephen W. Durrant, eds. (2000). *The Siren and the Sage: Knowledge and Wisdom in Ancient Greece and China*. London: Cassell.

Shankman, Stephen, and Durrant, Stephen W., eds. (2002). *Early China/Ancient Greece: Thinking through Comparisons*. Albany: State University of New York Press.

Shaw, Ian, ed. (2000). *The Oxford History of Ancient Egypt*. Oxford: Oxford University Press.

*Shiji* 史記. (1962). By Sima Qian司馬遷. Beijing: Zhonghua shuju.

Simpson, William K. (1970). "A Late Old Kingdom Letter to the Dead from Nag' Ed-Deir N 3500." *Journal of Egyptian Archaeology*, vol. 56: 58–64.

Sinclair, Andrew. (1967). *The Greek Anthology*. New York: Macmillan.

Sturdwick, Nigel C. (2005). *Texts from the Pyramid Age*. Atlanta: Society of Biblical Literature.

Sun Zuoyun 孫作雲. (1977). "Loyang XiHan Bu Qianqiu mu bihua kaoshi洛陽西漢卜千秋墓壁畫考釋." *Wenwu* 文物, vol. 6: 17–22.

Taylor, J. B. (2010). *Ancient Egyptian Book of the Dead*. London: British Museum.

Trigger, Bruce G. (2003). *Understanding Early Civilizations: A Comparative Study.* Cambridge: Cambridge University Press.

Tseng, Lilian L. Y. (2011). *Picturing Heaven in Early China.* Cambridge, MA: Harvard University Press.

Walsem, René van. (2008). *Mastabas: A Research Tool for the Study of the Secular or "Daily Life" Scenes and Their Accompanying Texts in the Elite Tombs of the Memphite Area in the Old Kingdom* (CD-ROM). Leuven: Peeters.

Wang Chong 王充. (1990). *Lunheng jijie.* 論衡集解. Commented by Liu Pansui 劉盼遂. Taipei: Shijie shuju.

Wang Donglin王東林, and Wang Guan王冠, eds. (2016). *Tushuo Haihunhou 2: Liu He qimu*圖說海昏侯2劉賀其墓. Jiangxi meishu chubanshe江西美術出版社.

Wang Fu 王符. (1971). *Qianfulun* 潛夫論. Taipei: Zhonghua Shuju.

Wang, Eugene Y. (2011). "Ascend to Heaven or Stay in the Tomb? Paintings in Mawangdui Tomb 1 and the Virtual Ritual of Revival in Second-Century BCE China." In *Mortality in Traditional Chinese Thought,* eds. Philip J. Ivanhoe and Amy Olberding, 37–84. Albany: State University of New York Press.

Wang Xianqien 王先謙. (1971). *Xunzi jijie*荀子集解. Taipei: Shijie shuju.

Wang, Zhongshu. (1982). *Han civilization.* New Haven: Yale University Press.

Watson, Burton. (1963). *Hsün Tzu.* New York: Columbia University Press.

Watson, Burton. (1964). *Chuang Tzu, basic writings.* New York: Columbia University Press.

Watson, Burton. (1967). *Basic Writings of Mo Tzu, Hsun Tzu, and Han Fei Tzu.* New York: Columbia University Press.

Watson, Burton. (1974). *Courtier and Commoner in Ancient China.* New York: Columbia University Press.

Watson, James L., and Evelin S. Rawski, eds. (1988). *Death Ritual in Late Imperial and Modern China.* Berkeley: University of California Press.

Wente, Edward. (1990). *Letters from Ancient Egypt.* Atlanta: Scholar Press.

Wenwu chubanshe. (1973). *Changsha Chumu bohua* 長沙楚墓帛畫. Beijing: Wenwu chubanshe.

Wierzbica, Anna. (2004). "Happiness in Cross-linguistic and Cross-cultural perspective." *Daedalus,* vol. 133, no. 2: 34–43.

Wilkinson, Richard H., and Kent R. Weeks, eds. (2016). *The Oxford Handbook of the Valley of the Kings.* Oxford: Oxford University Press.

Wu Hung. (1992). "Art in a Ritual Context: Rethinking Mawangdui." *Early China,* vol. 17: 111–44.

Wu Hung. (2010). *The Art of the Yellow Springs: Understanding Chinese Tombs.* London: Reaktion.

Wu Wenling 鄔文玲. (2015). "Du Fangmatan Qinjian zhiguai gushi zhaji讀放馬灘秦簡志怪故事札記." *Guoxue xuekan*國學學刊, vol. 4: 13–17.

Xin, Li-xiang 信立祥. (2008). *Handai Huaxiangshi Zonghe Yanjiu* 汉代画像石综合研究. Beijing: Wenwu.

Xing, Yitian 邢義田. (1986). "The Development of Han Murals and Tombs of Murals 漢代壁畫的發展和壁畫墓." *Bulletin of the Institute of History and Philology Academia Sinica*, vol. 57, no. 1: 139–70.

Yu, Ying-shih. (1987). "O Soul Come Back! A Study in the Changing Conceptions of the Soul and Afterlife in Pre-Buddhist China." *Harvard Journal of Asiatic Studies*, vol. 47, no. 2: 363–95.

Žabkar, Louis V. (1968). *A Study of the Ba Concept in Ancient Egyptian Texts*. Chicago: University of Chicago Press.

Zandee, Jan. (1960). *Death as an Enemy*. Leiden: Brill.

Zeng, Zhaoyu 曾昭燏 Jiang, Baogeng 蔣寶庚 and Li, Zhongyi 黎忠義 eds. (1956). *Yinan guhuaxiangshimu fajuebaogao* 沂南古畫像石墓發掘報告. Beijing: State Administration of Cultural Heritage, Ministry of Culture.

Zhang, Xunliao 張勛燎, and Bai, Bin 白彬. (2006). "DongHan muzang chutu jiezhu qi he tienshidao de qiyuan 東漢墓葬出土解注器和天師道的起源." In *Zhongguo Daojiao kaogu* 中國道教考古, eds. Zhang Xunliao and Bai Bin, 1–332. Beijing: Xianzhuang shuju.

Zhang, Zhenglang 張政烺. (1981). "Aichengshu ding shiwen 哀成叔鼎釋文." *Guwenzi yanjiu* 古文字研究, vol. 5: 27–33.

Zheng, Yan 鄭岩. (2013). *Masking Death: Funerary Art of Medieval China* 逝者的面具：漢唐墓葬藝術研究. Beijing: Peking University Press.

Zhongguo kexueyuan kaogu yenjiuso 中国科学院考古研究所. (1959). *Loyang shaogou hanmu* 洛陽燒溝漢墓. Beijing: Kexue chubanshe.

Zhongguo shehui kexue kaogu yanjiusuo 中國社會科學院考古研究所, and Hebeisheng wenwu guanlichu 河北省文物管理處. (1980). *Mancheng Hanmu fajue baogao* 滿城漢墓發掘報告. Beijing: Wenwu.

Zhou Fengwu 周鳳五. (2001). "Jiudian Chujian gao Wu Yi chongtan." 九店楚簡告武夷重探, *Zhongyang yanjiuyuan lishi yuyan yanjiusuo jikan* 中央研究院歷史語言研究所集刊, vol. 72, no. 4: 943–5.

*Zhuangzi jishi* 莊子集釋. (1985). By Guo Qingfan 郭慶藩. Beijing: Zhonghua shuju.

Zongguo huaxiangshi quanji bianji weiyuanhui 中國畫像石全集編輯委員會. (1997). *Zongguo huaxiangshi quanji* 中國畫像石全集, 8 vols. Zhengzhou: Henan Meishu Chubanshe.

*Zuozhuan zhengyi* 左傳正義. (1976). In *Shisanjingzhushu* 十三經注疏. By Ruan Yuan 阮元. Taipei: Yiwen chubanshe.

# Index

Abydos 15
"Admonitions of Ipuwer" 97–8
adult tombs 23. *See also* tombs
afterlife. *See also* life after death
   anxiety concerning 2
   in China 73
   death and 10, 143
   Egyptian social ethics in 88–98, 136
   existence of 136
   people's attitude toward 33
*akh* 9, 66
Akhethotep Hemi/Nebkauhor at Saqqara 40, 89
ancient China (*c*. 1600 BCE-220 CE) 1, 5–7
   evolution of burial styles in 22–33
   search for happiness in 135–6
ancient Egypt
   belief in netherworld 1
   comparative study 2, 6
   evolution of burial style in 14–22
   foreigners in 7
   hope, fear, and happiness in 110–16
   search for happiness in 135–6
*Ancient Egypt and Early China: State, Society, and Culture* (Barbieri-Low) 7
Ankhmeryremeryptah 90, 91
Anubis 20, 34, 65, 83, 89
appeal to the living 114
Assmann, Jan 87
Aswan 18
Autumn period 26, 32, 98, 125

*ba* 9, 95
Bai Bin 129, 131
Barbieri-Low, Anthony J. 7
Bárta, M. 20–1
Beautiful West 5, 11, 61, 72, 88, 106, 144
belief
   about life 2
   of Chinese 8, 136
   of Egyptians 8, 88–98
   in netherworld 1, 3
   religious 2, 6, 12, 87, 90, 96, 135, 136
   social grouping and social status 14
Beni Hassan 17–18
biographical inscriptions 119
*Book of Ceremony* (I-li) 141
*Book of Odes* 73
*Book of Rites (Liji)* 35, 108
*Book of the Dead* 4, 5, 20, 39, 44, 46, 69–72, 85, 87, 91, 93, 95, 104, 114–17, 120, 133, 137, 142
Buddhism 5, 9, 82
   China before 8, 90
bureaucracy 79, 81, 83, 84, 98, 137, 143
   Egypt 137
burial/cemeteries
   customs 3, 32
   Egyptians belief of 4
   funerary ceremony 10
   inclusion of water jars in 14
   prehistorical 14–15
Byzantium 8

Cai Zhi 80–1
Cao Bolu family 132
*carpe diem* 119
Chavannes, E. 5
China
   belief in existence of soul 2
   before Buddhism 8, 90
   bureaucracy 137
   foreigners in 7
   pre-Buddhist 5
   Shang Dynasty 34
   tomb paintings 59
Christianity in Rome 8
*Chuci (Songs of the South)* 74–5, 126, 138
*Coffin Texts* 4, 44, 46, 69–72, 95, 112, 120, 137
*Commentary of Zuo (Zuozhuan* 左傳) 36
commonality of humanity 3

Confucian 58, 90, 99–102, 108, 121–3, 125, 132, 140–1
*Confucian Analect* 100, 122, 123
Confucius 11, 36, 58, 121, 123
*Controller of Fate* (Siming) 75, 78, 98, 136
Cretans 41
cultural landscape 143

*dao* 87
Daoism 9, 58, 82, 99–100, 130–1, 139–41, 143–4
Daoist talisman 130
Dark City *(Youdu)* 5, 74–5
Dawenkou culture 23
deep mourning 139
desirable life 124
*ding* 26
*Discourse on Salt and Iron (Yantielun)* 102
"Dispute between a Man and His Ba" 97–8
Duke Mu of Qin 36
Duke Wen of Jin 36
Duke Zhuang 74
"Duties of the Vizier" 62
Dynasty 0 (*c.* 3300–2950 BCE) 15

early China
  imagination of world after death in 6
  mortuary customs 121
  tomb style in 46, 73
Early Dynastic period (First and Second Dynasties, *c.* 2950–2775 BCE) 15–16, 33
Eastern Han (*c.* 1700 BCE-300 CE) 9, 31, 42, 51, 78, 104, 118, 129
Eastern Zhou 25, 74
Egypt 6
  bureaucracy 137
  foreigners in 7
  funerary texts 137
  graphic representations in tombs 37–46
  history of 4, 112
  religious beliefs 2
  religious texts 137
  social ethics in afterlife 88–98
  texts 12, 109, 116–21
Egyptian Ushabti 7
Egyptologists 9
Eighteenth Dynasty tombs 96
El-Hagarsa 18
Emperor Jing 28

Emperor Wen of Han (203–157 BCE) d 139–40
Emperor Wu (156–87 BCE) 80, 102
Epicurus 124
ethics
  Confucian 99
  morality 58
  social 68, 87, 92, 107, 136
  values 88, 89, 91, 138
exorcistic text. *See* tomb quelling texts
"extended face-down" 23
"extended face-up" 23

fear
  in ancient Egypt 110–16
  Egyptian texts 116–21
  eradication of 109
Field of Offerings 4, 43, 61, 70–2, 85, 112, 114, 120
Field of Rushes 4, 67, 69, 70, 82, 83, 114
Fifth Dynasty 21–2
filial piety 99, 100, 102, 132
First Intermediate Period 96–7
Fu Hao 24
funerary culture 22
funerary objects 13–14, 99, 101, 103, 104, 127, 129, 133
funerary rituals 2, 10, 40, 68, 71, 72, 100
funerary texts 61, 64
  China 83
  Egypt 72, 137
  Han 81, 99, 137
  Old Kingdom 61, 65
  Osiris 71

ghosts 5, 76, 98, 125
Giza Plateau 18, 20
Gongsun Qiang 75
Greco-Roman 7
Greece 7
Greek Ptolemaic Dynasty 120
*gui* 26
Gu Yanwu 5

Hai Hun 28
Han Chinese, graphic representations 46–58
Han Dynasty 5, 22, 27, 29, 34, 36, 81, 101
  funerary texts 137
  imagination 138

Mawangdui tomb no. 1 44
Texts 73–82
tombs 7, 105, 113
happiness 1–6
  in ancient Egypt 110–16
  blissfulness and 50
  desire for 136
  in early Chinese texts 121–33
  idea of 1, 6, 109, 121, 138
Harper's Song 96, 97, 110, 111, 119, 143
Hathor (goddess) 113
Hayes, W. C. 38
*he* 26
Heavenly Emperor 79, 130, 132
heavenly officials 128
Heavenly Sire *(tiangong)* 78
hedonistic 111
hell 142–3
Herb of Life 128
Holinger tomb 57
hope, ancient Egypt 110–16
"horizon dwellers" 69
house of eternity *(pr n nḥḥ)* 33, 62, 64, 110
Hou Yi 49
*hu* 26
Huainanzi 99
*huangchang ticou* 28
humanity 12, 37
  commonality of 3
human sacrifice 24–5, 36, 73
hun 79, 130

iconographic representations 37–60
  graphic representations in Egyptian tombs 37–46
  Han Chinese graphic representations 46–58
Idu 112
Iki 110
*imakhu* (blessed one) 14, 34, 65, 88, 89, 91, 108
immortal 128
*Instruction Addressed to Kagemni* 94
*The Instruction Addressed to King Merikare* 94
*Instruction of Amenemope* 95
*Instruction of Any* 95, 115, 116
*The Instruction of Hardjedef* 94, 114
Isenkhebe 117

Jewish Sheol 74
Jiang Ji 81–2
Jiangsu Province 28
Jilu 123, 124
joy 122, 126

*ka* 9, 19–20, 40
Khentyimentyu 89
King Cheng 35
King Cheops 142
King Father of the West 127–8
King Kang 35
King Tutankhamun 106
King Wu Ding 24

Lady Dai 26, 28, 47, 49
lamentation 139
*Land of Osiris* 91, 108, 110, 111, 114, 120
land-purchasing text *(maidi quan)* 132
Laozi 140
lead man 104
letter to the dead 63, 64, 89, 112
*li* 100, 107
Lichtheim, M. 4, 93
life after death 1–2, 11, 14, 32, 34, 84, 106, 109, 120, 127, 143. *See also* afterlife
Liu He 28
Liu Sheng 28
*lizhi* 130
longevity 127, 128
Lord Earth (Tu Bo) 74
*Lord of the Underworld* (Dixiazhu) 136
Lucretius 124

*maat* 87, 89, 91, 93, 97
Majiayao culture 23
Marquis Dai 26–7, 47
Marquis Qi 100
mastaba 15–20, 33–4, 39
  Egyptian 47
  structural changes 21
Mawangdui 51
  paintings 46–55
  silk paintings 128
  tombs 105
*Maximum of Ptahhotep* 93–4
Mengzi 121–2, 123
Mereri 113
Mereruka, tomb of 19
Meresankh, tomb of 19

Mesopotamia 7, 74
Middle Kingdom 18, 39, 93, 94, 110, 143
Mid-Yellow River Longshan culture 23
Minoans 41, 57
mirror inscriptions 128, 129
model of a slaughterhouse 45
Mont Tai 5
*mouli* 130
Mount Buzhou 76
Mount Tai 80, 130–1

Naqada I Amratian culture cemetery 15
Nebkauhor 40, 89
Neferhotep 110
Neolithic period 22
Neolithic Yang-shao culture 23
netherworld
  bureaucracy 137, 142
  changing imagination of 34
  Chinese ethical values about 98–103, 107, 143, 144
  conceptualization of 133, 135
  death and life in 110, 116
  deities in 113, 137, 138, 142
  Egyptian perceptions of 22, 135, 141, 142
  happy life in 120, 143, 144
  in modern scholarship 5
  predominant tradition about 112
  Zhuangzi's portrayal of 126
New Kingdom 18, 22, 39, 93, 95, 115, 142
New Kingdom Egypt 7
non-Confucian 58

offering list 14, 44–5
Old Kingdom 14, 20, 33, 39, 42, 61, 89, 94, 96, 142
  Egyptians in 93
  ethical values from 91
  rock-cut tombs 18
Osiris 66, 71, 87, 90, 93–5, 106, 136–7, 142–3

painted brick tombs 56–8
paradise 83, 118, 120, 126, 135, 136, 137, 142
paraphernalia 3, 35, 51, 80, 107, 133, 141
personal piety 96
pessimism, in Egyptian texts 110–16
pharaohs 28
Pharaonic period (*c.* 3000–300 BCE) 1, 9

*po* 79, 130
poetic expression 110
political-moral authority 102
postmortem punishment 106
prejudice 7
Pre-Qin 73–82
Ptah 119
Ptahhotep 58, 94, 95, 97
Ptolemaic Dynasty 118, 120
Ptolemaic period 119
*Pyramid Texts* 4, 21, 65–9, 120, 137

Qiance (遣策) 44
Qijia culture 23
Qin Dynasty: 221–207 BCE 75, 139
Qin–Han periods (221 BCE to 220 CE) 127, 137
Queen Mother of the West 49, 56, 128, 129
Qu Yuan 74

racial difference 7
Ramesside period 95, 96
rectangular vertical pit 23
Reisner, George A. 33
relief figures 19
religious texts 4, 11–12, 66, 109, 137
resurrection 98, 133
rock-cut tombs 18–19, 21–2, 28, 29, 34, 39, 42, 47, 64
Roman Empire 7
Rome, Christianity in 8
royal tombs 15–16, 21–2, 24–5, 28, 33, 39, 42, 73
Ru 121

Saqqara 15, 16, 18
self-cultivation 121, 123, 144
Semites 57
Seny 112
*serdab* 17
Shandong Longshan culture 23
Shangdang 79, 130
Shang Dynasty 22, 23, 32, 34–5, 73
shang-fang 128
Shang Royal burial 25
*Shipwrecked Sailor* 142
*Shujing (Book of History)* 80
silk painting 47, 49, 51–5, 128
Sixth Dynasty 21, 34, 89, 90, 137
skepticism 36, 97, 112, 136

social convention 32, 87, 98, 101, 125, 127
social ethics in afterlife 88–98
social life 3
social norms 1, 103
Solon 126, 144
"the Son of Heaven" 140
"Son of Ra" 140
soul 88, 89, 91, 116, 126, 129, 132, 138, 143
Spring period 26, 32, 98, 125
Stoics 121
Sui Shaoyan 84
"Supreme Happiness" (*Zhuangzi*) 124
surrogate objects 13–14
Syrians 41

Taimhotep 119
*Tale of the Two Brothers* 142
Tang Empires 8
textual representations 61–85
  Book of the Dead 69–72
  *Coffin Texts* 69–72
  in Netherworld 61–5
  in Pre-Qin and Han Texts 73–82
  *Pyramid Texts* 65–9
Third Dynasty 16, 21, 34, 37
"37 Asiatics coming" 41
thrifty burial 99, 101, 102, 116, 141
Thutmosis III 62
Tianfeng reign 128
tomb
  of Akhethotep Hemi/Nebkauhor 40
  of Bu Qianqiu 55
  of Fu Hao 24, 25
  of Kaiemnefret (Fifth Dynasty) 62
  of Khnumhotep 41
  of Marquis Dai 47
  of Menkheperrasonb 41
  of Mereruka 19, 40
  of Metjen (Fourth Dynasty) 62
  quelling texts 78, 99, 129, 130, 131, 132
  of Rehkmire 62
  of Senmut 41
  of Senndjem 46
  of Thothrekh 118
  Xian 55
Trigger, Bruce 8
Twelfth Dynasty 41

Underground (*dixia*) 5
underworld 79, 130, 138
undesirable life 124
unpredictability, of God 96, 97
Upper Egypt 18
ushabti 103–5, 106, 107, 135

vertical shaft tomb 17

wall paintings 52
Wang Chong 103, 107
Wang Fu 50
Warring States period (476–221 BCE) 5, 7, 32–3, 35, 74, 75–6, 99, 127, 138, 141
Western Han 7, 30, 51, 56
  paintings 77
western paradise 97, 142–3
Western Thebes 18
Western Zhou 25
wisdom literature 7, 93, 95, 96, 114
wooden casket tomb 27
"world of the afterlife" 15
Wu Yi 77, 78

Xin Zhui 47
Xiwu 75
Xu Aqu 118, 129
Xunzi 13
Xu Wentai 130

Yang Wangsun 99–102, 141
*Yantielun* 102
Yellow God (Huangshen) 77, 78, 79, 83, 130, 132, 136
"Yellow God and the Big Dipper" (Huangshen beidou) 136
Yellow River 23
Yellow Spring (*Huangquan*) 5, 74, 80
Yungkang reign (167 CE) 127

Zenghou Yi 30
Zhang Xunliao 129, 131
Zhao Zi 35–6, 101
Zhou Dynasty 35
Zhuangzi 99, 124–7, 140, 144
Zi Gong 123
Ziqi 132
Zuozhuan 74, 98

www.ingramcontent.com/pod-product-compliance
Lightning Source LLC
Chambersburg PA
CBHW071934240426
43668CB00038B/1757